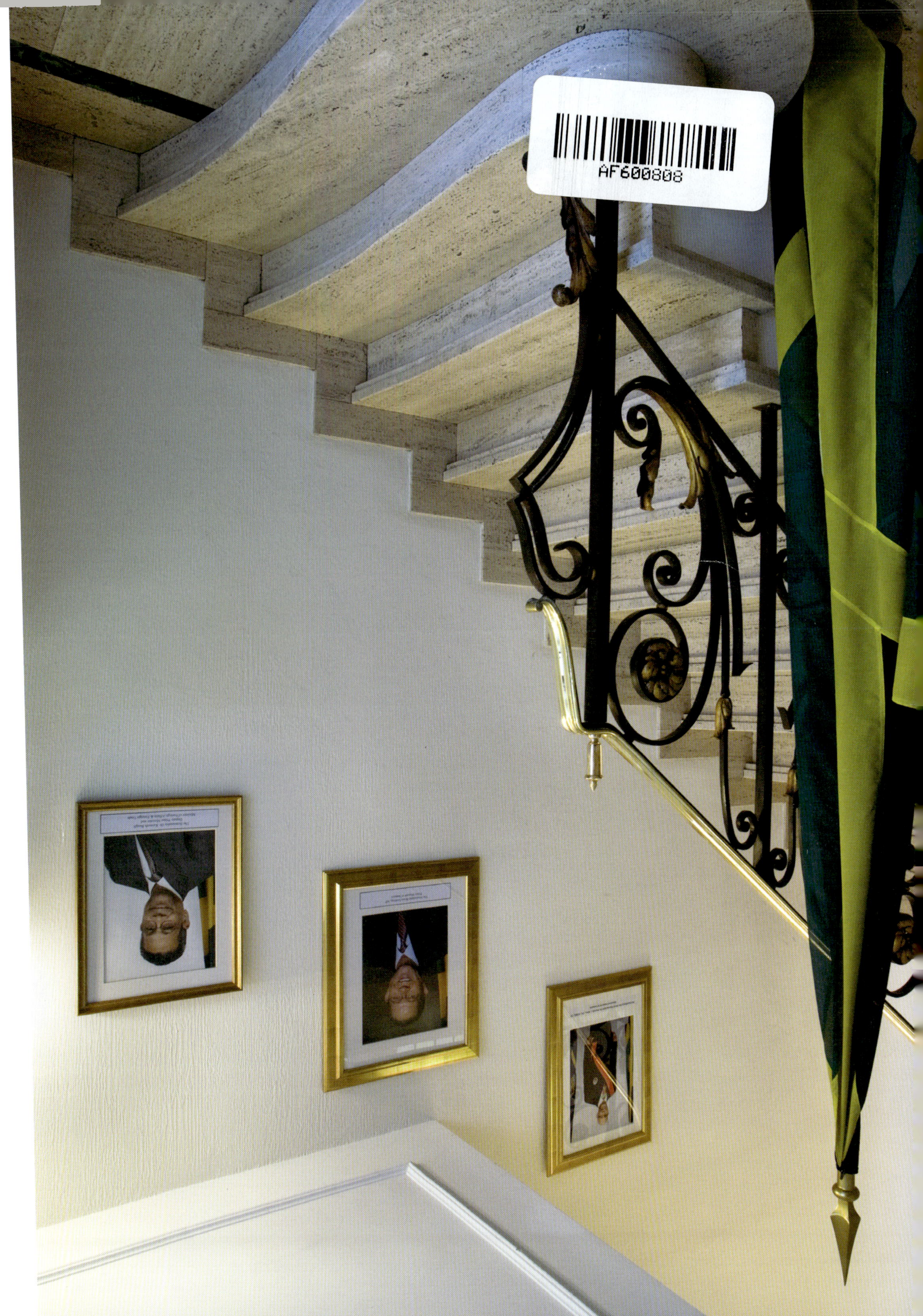

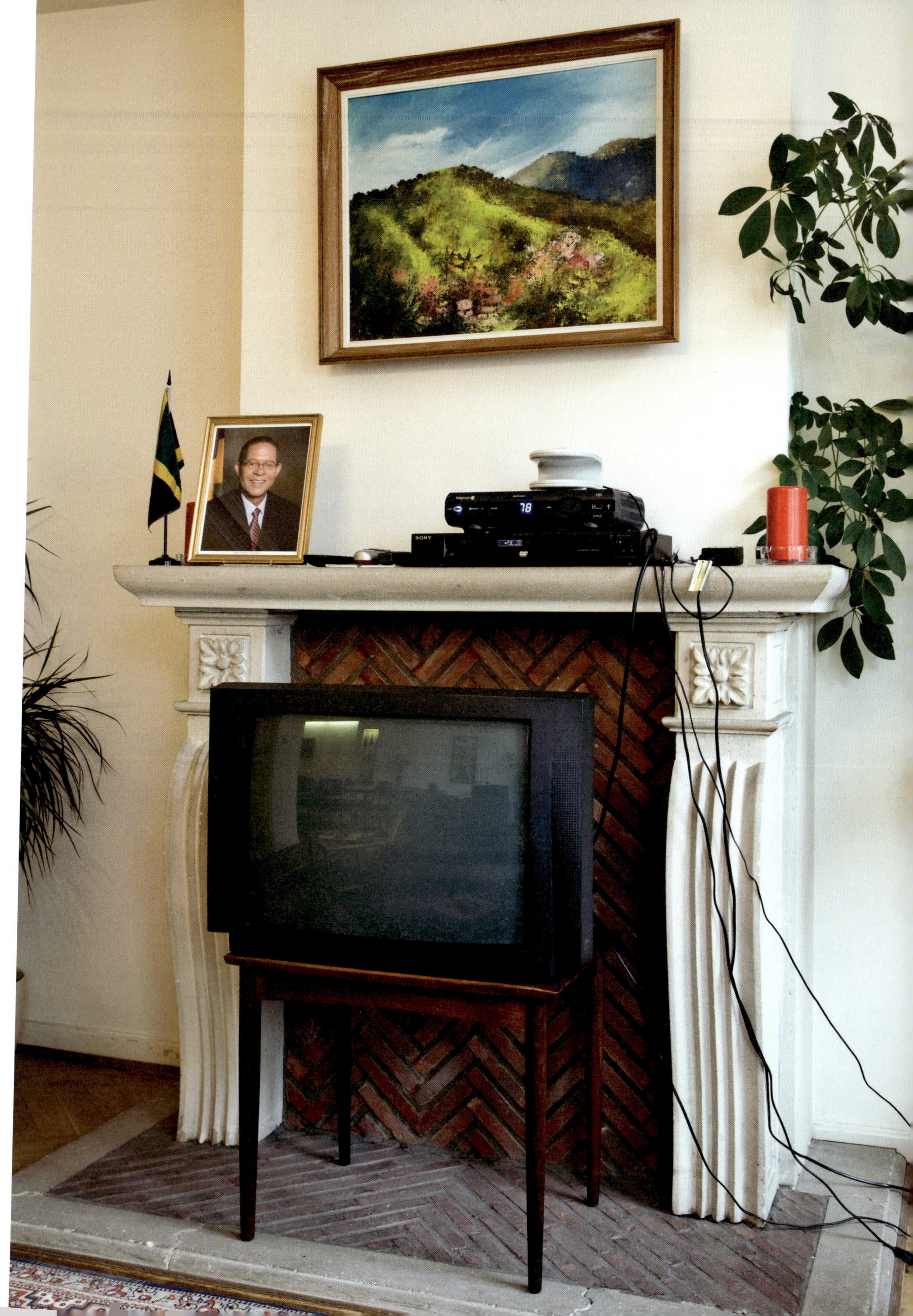
SONY
HD
78

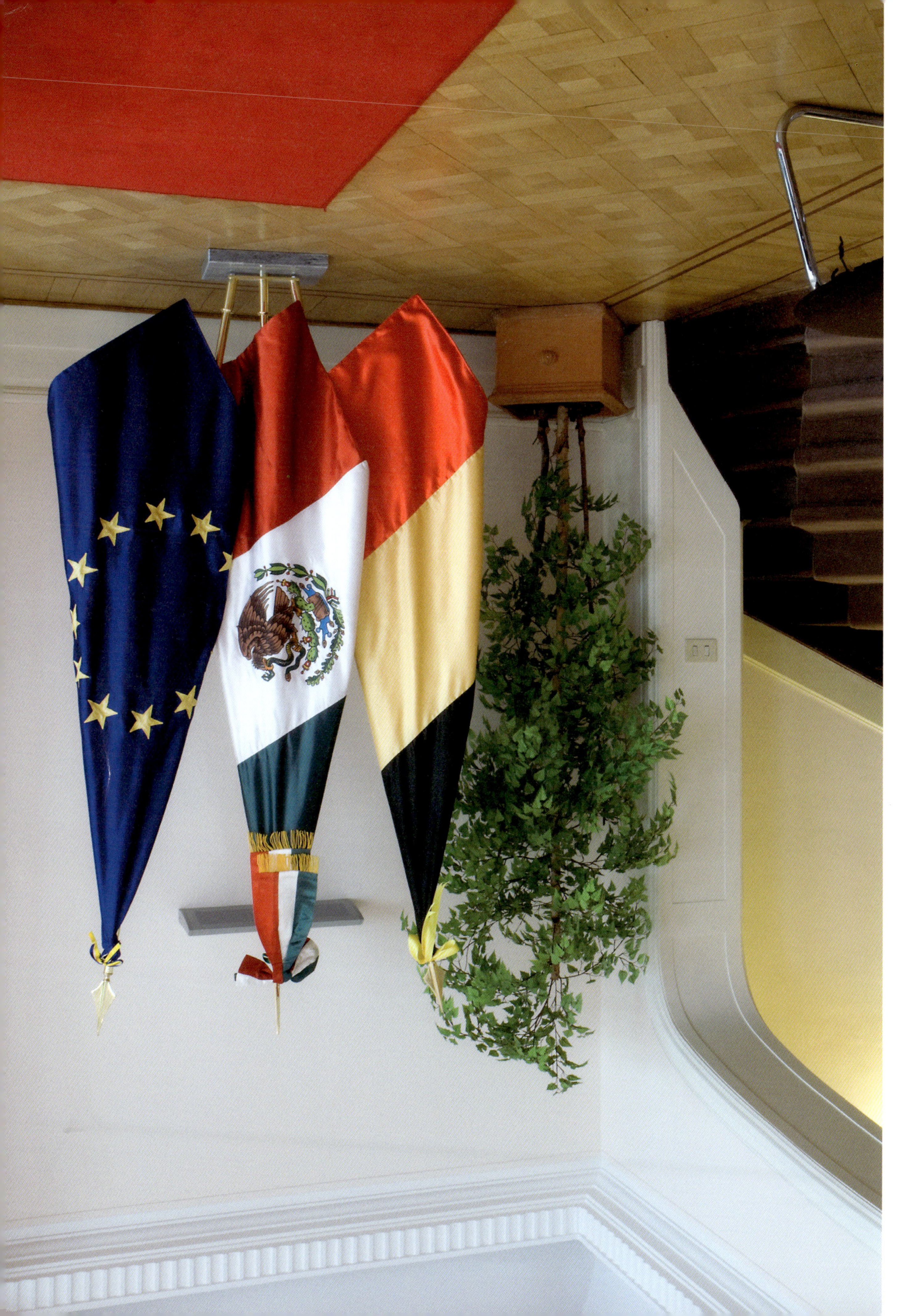

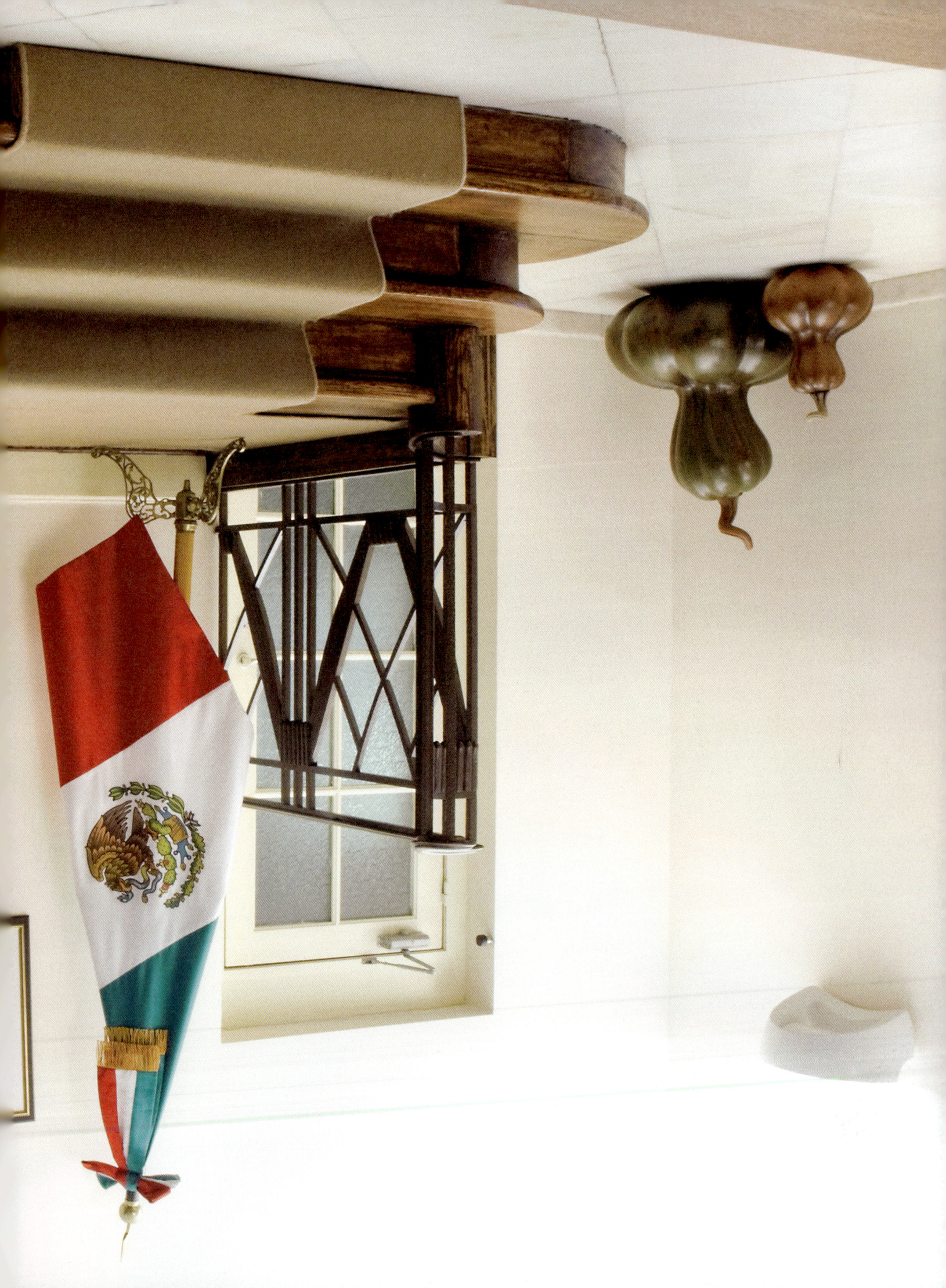

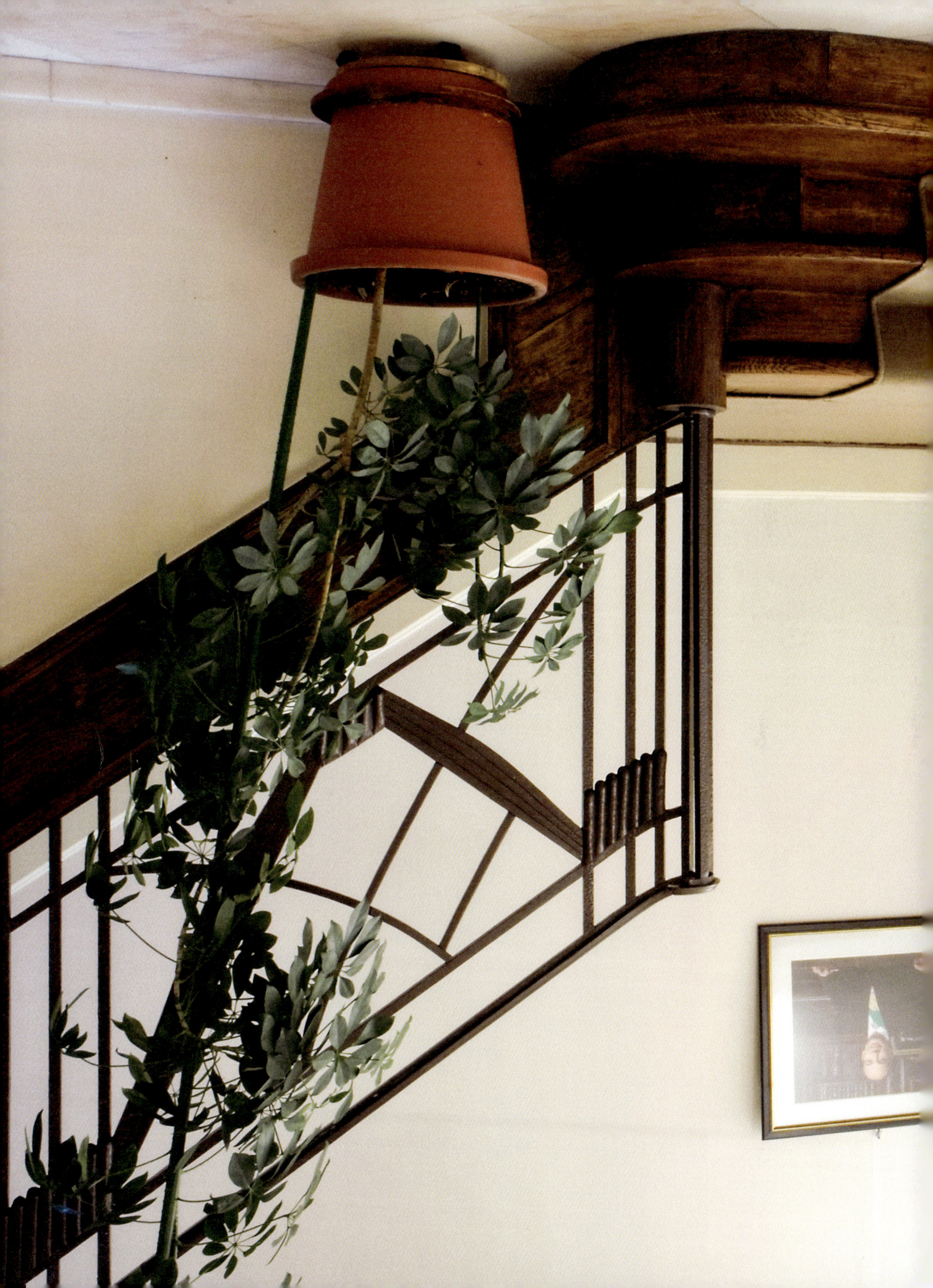

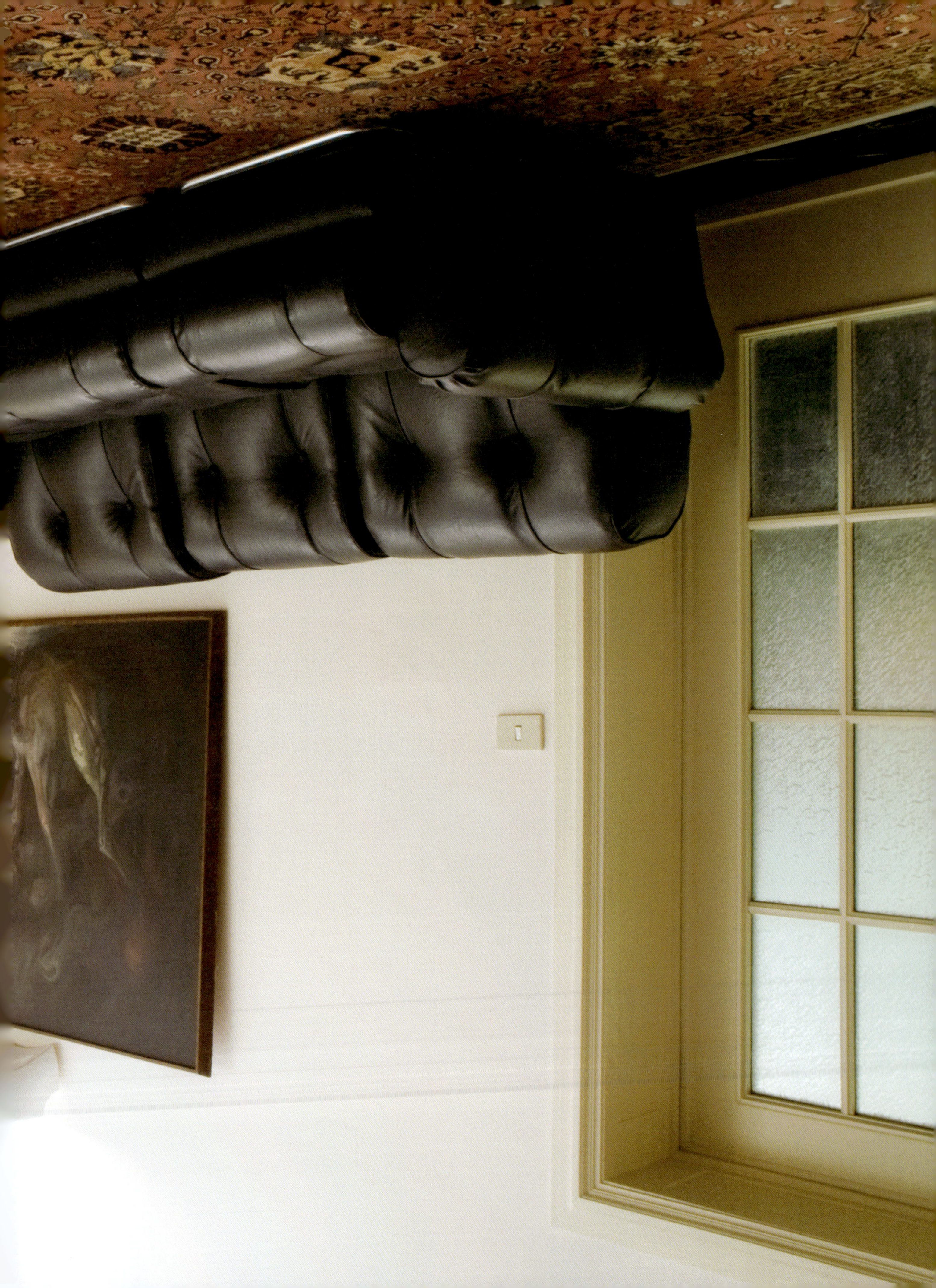

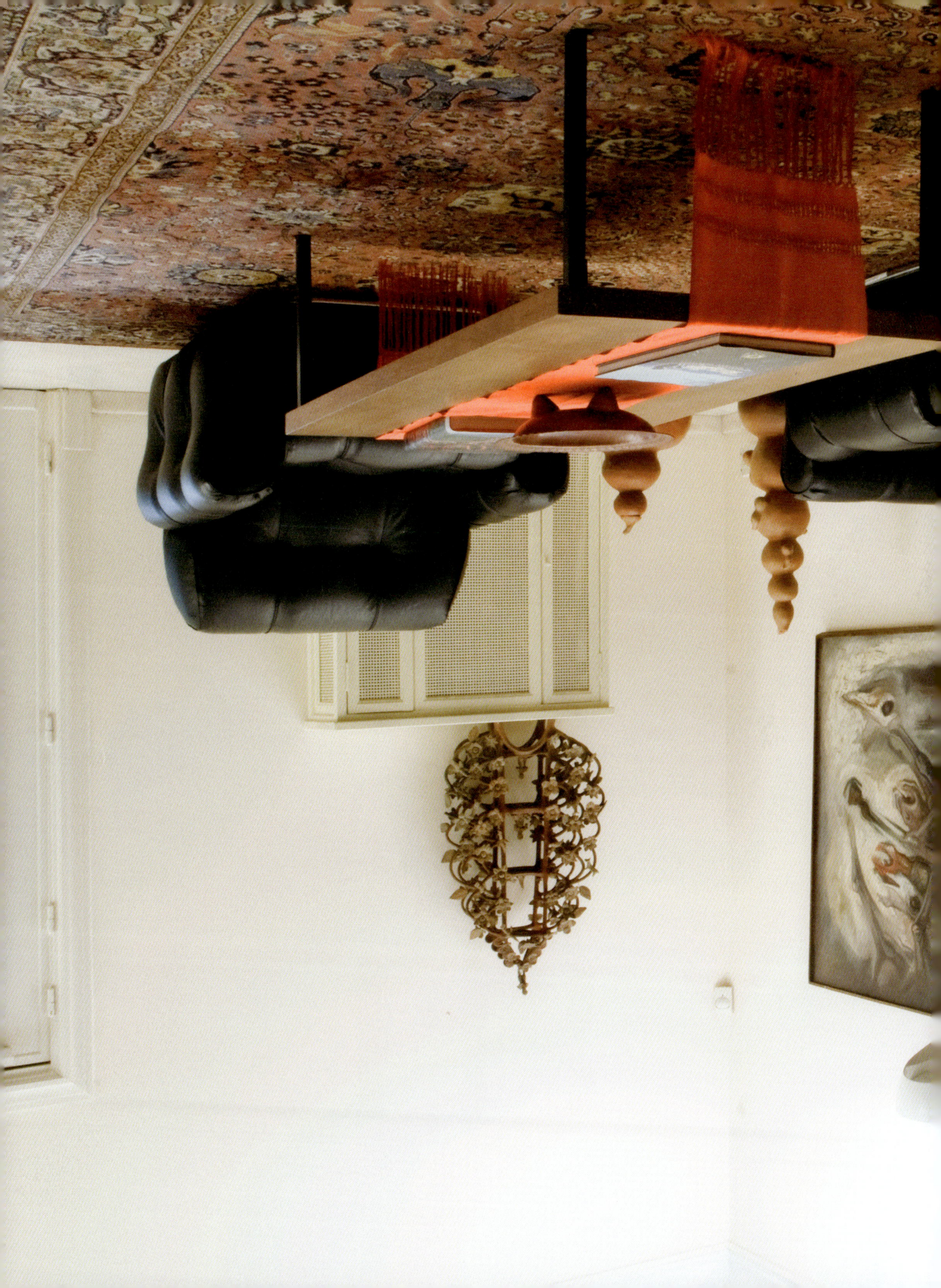

TR

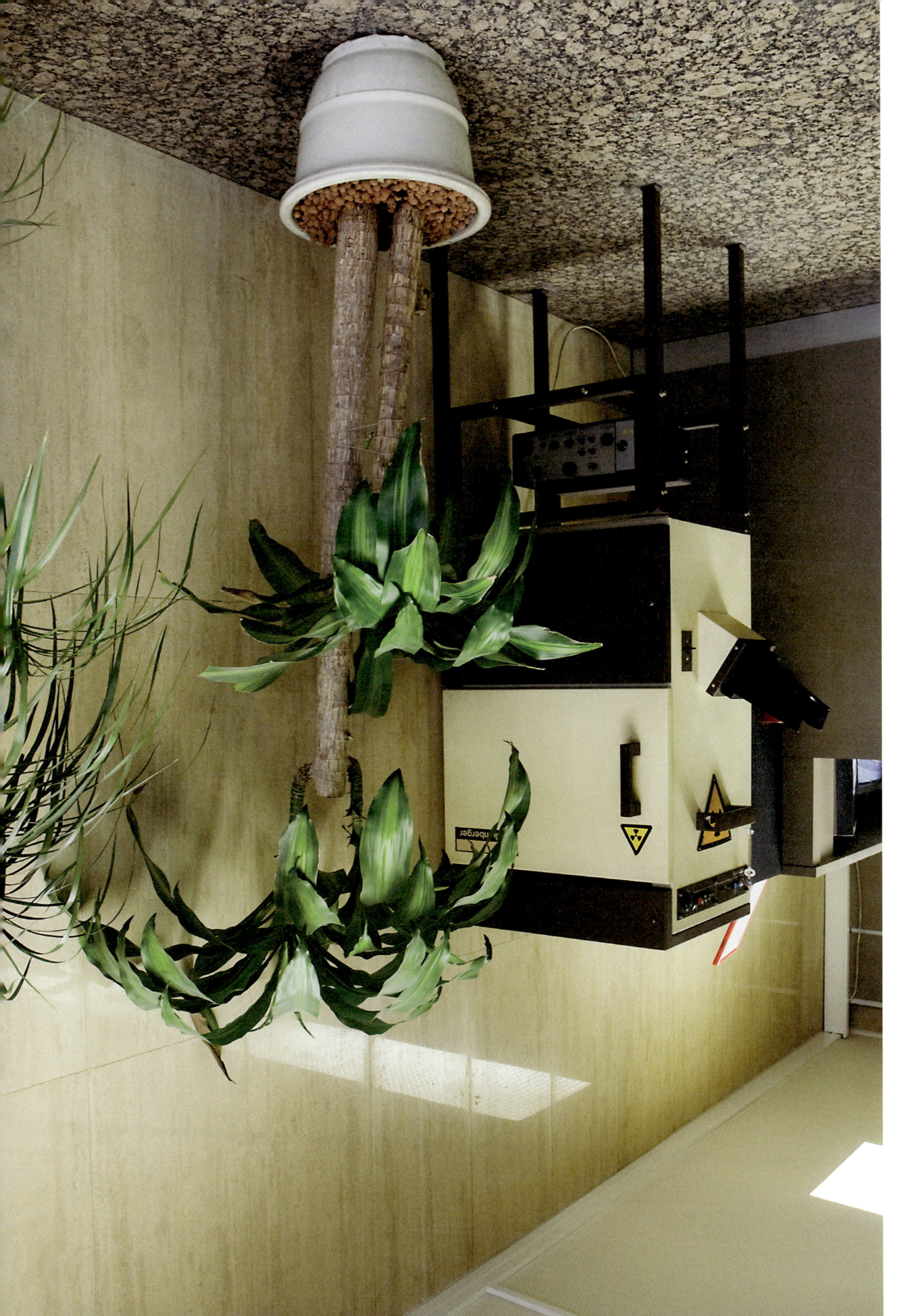

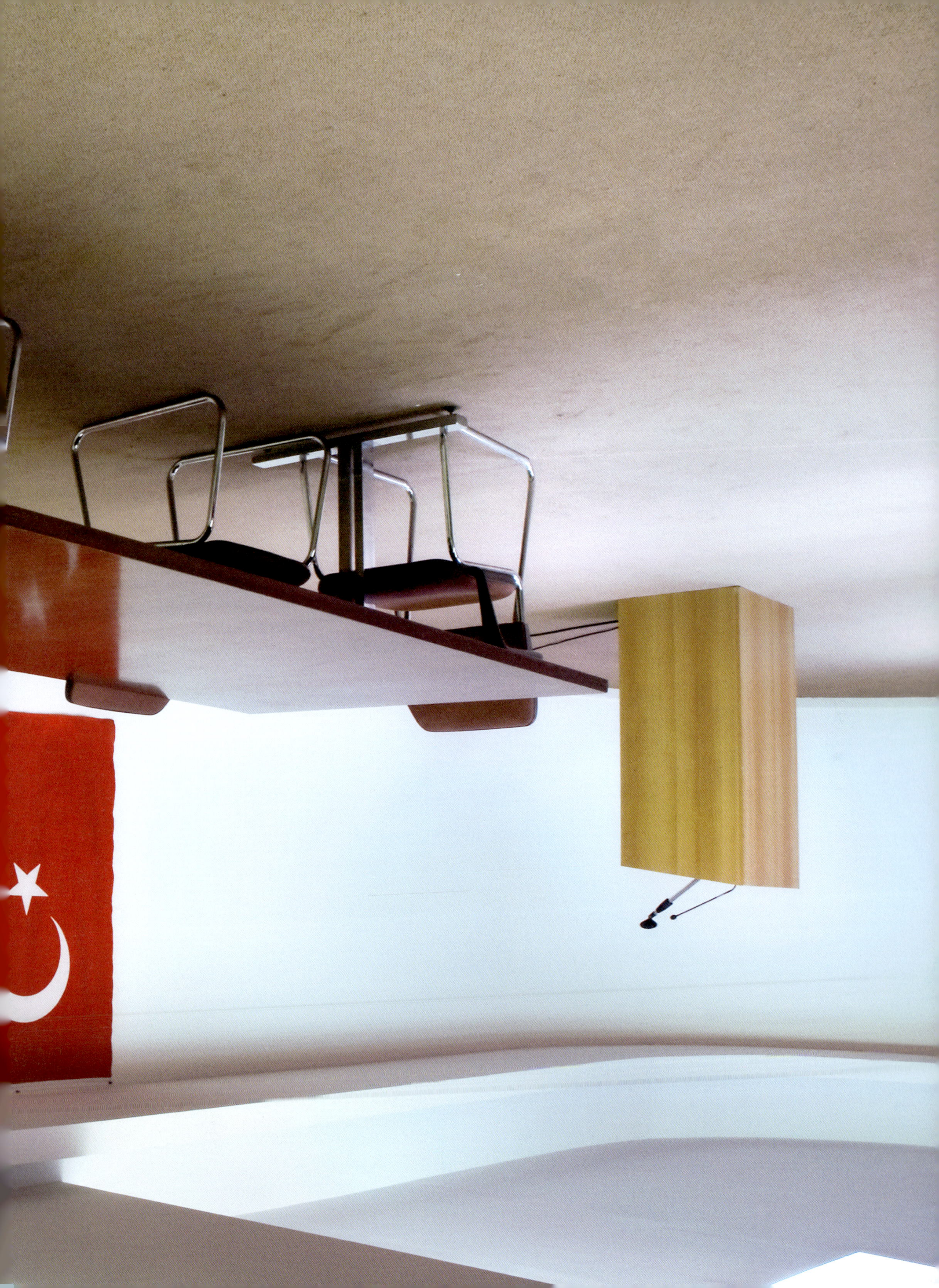

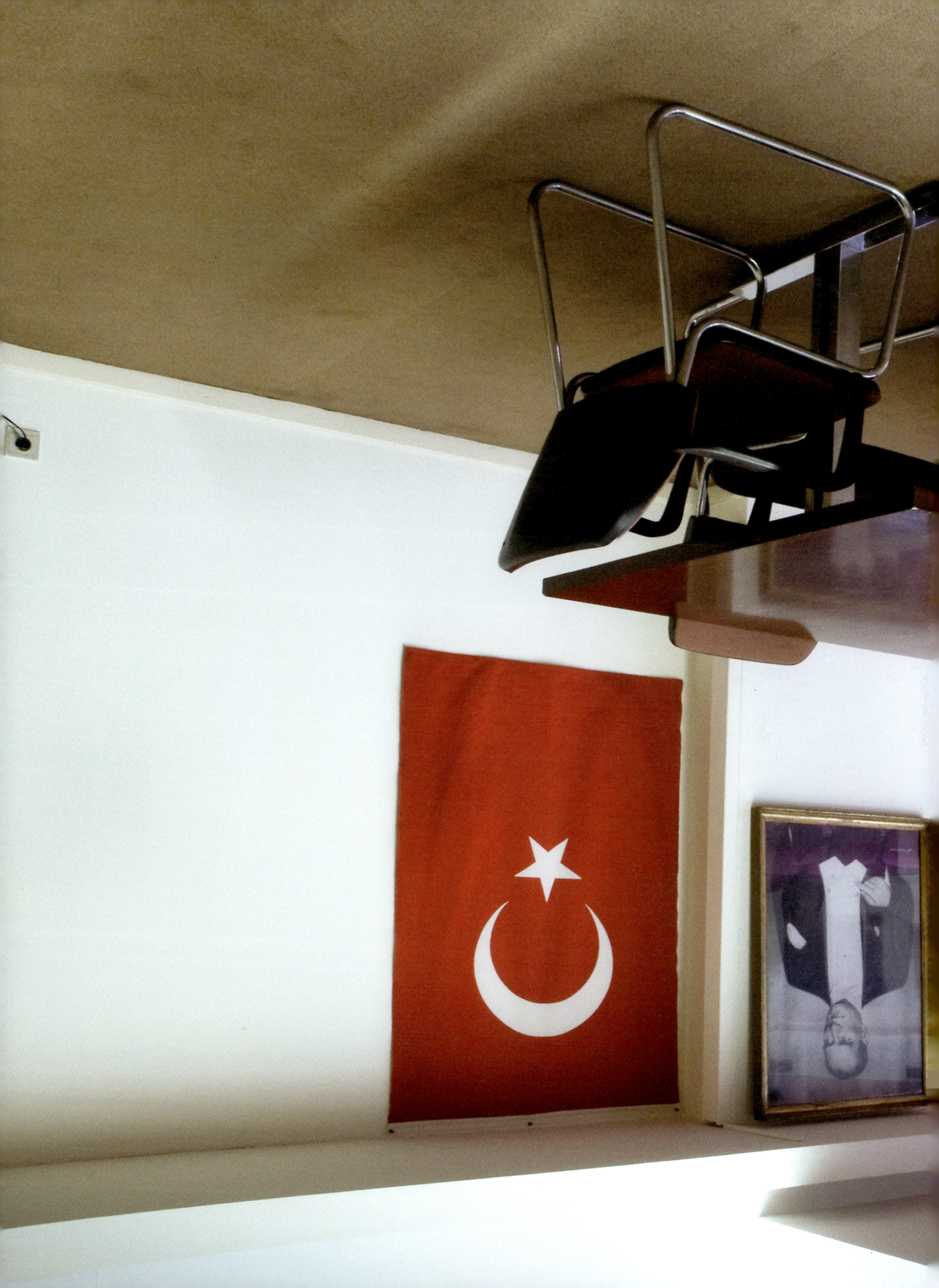

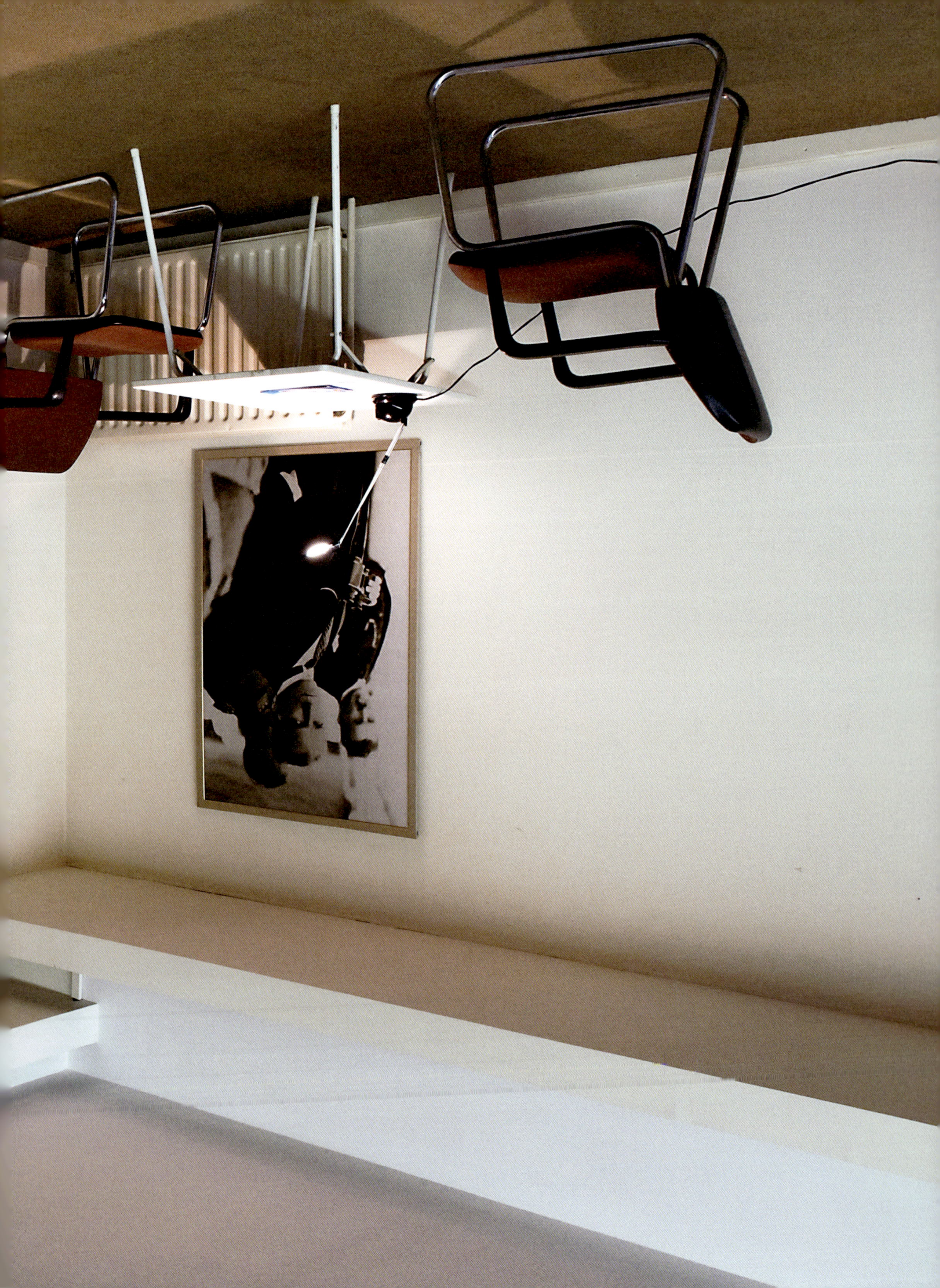

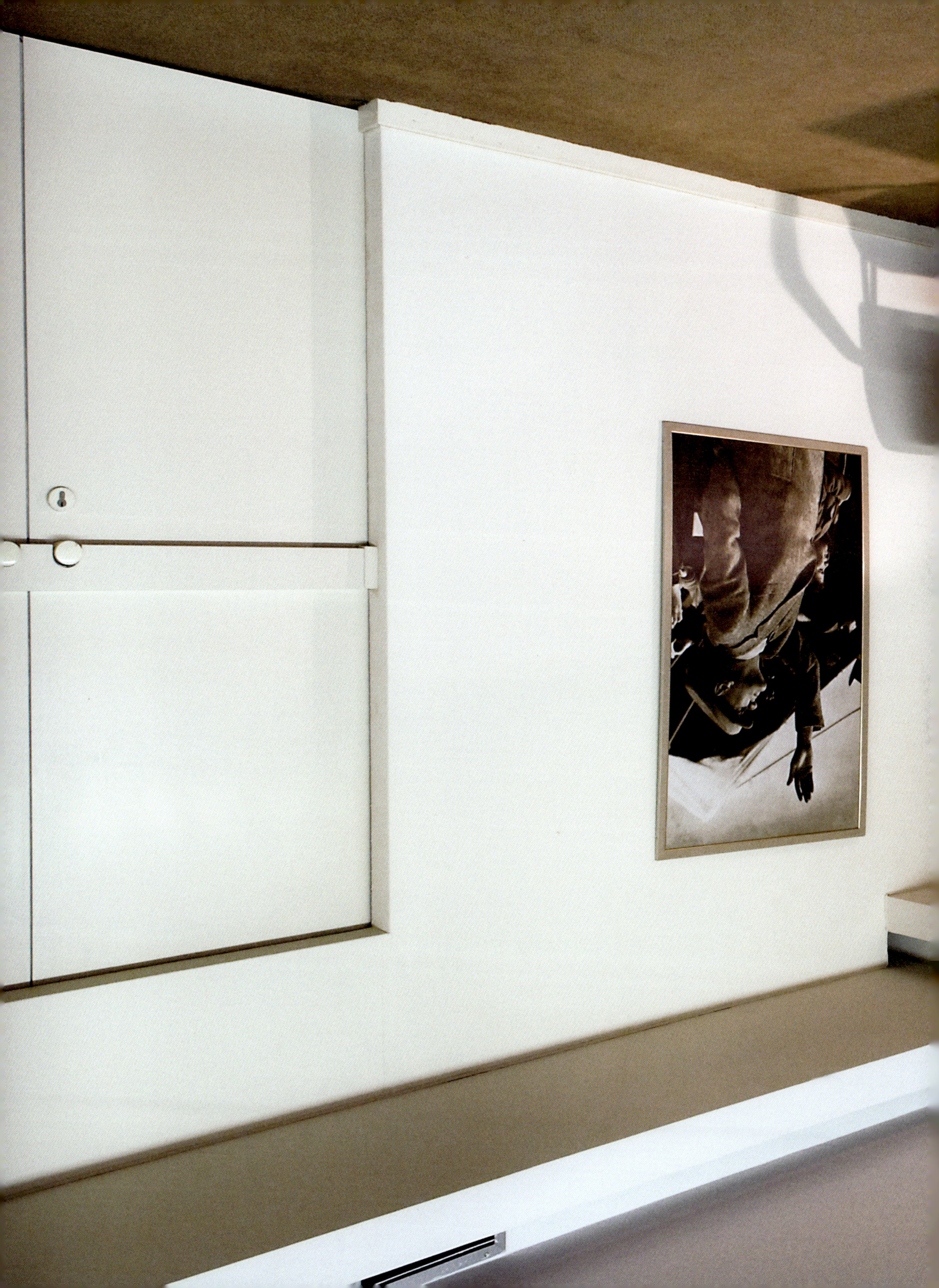

ZA

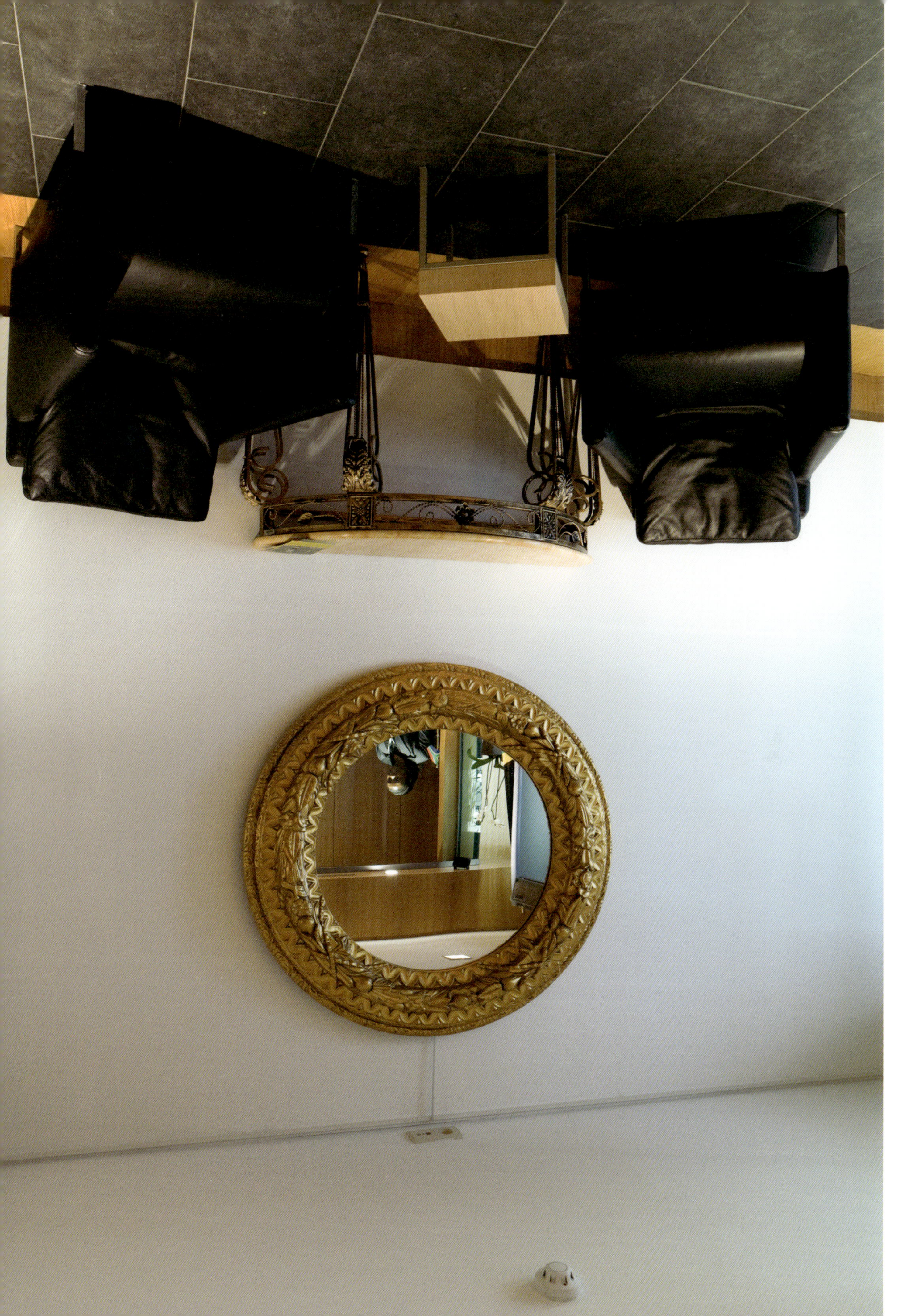

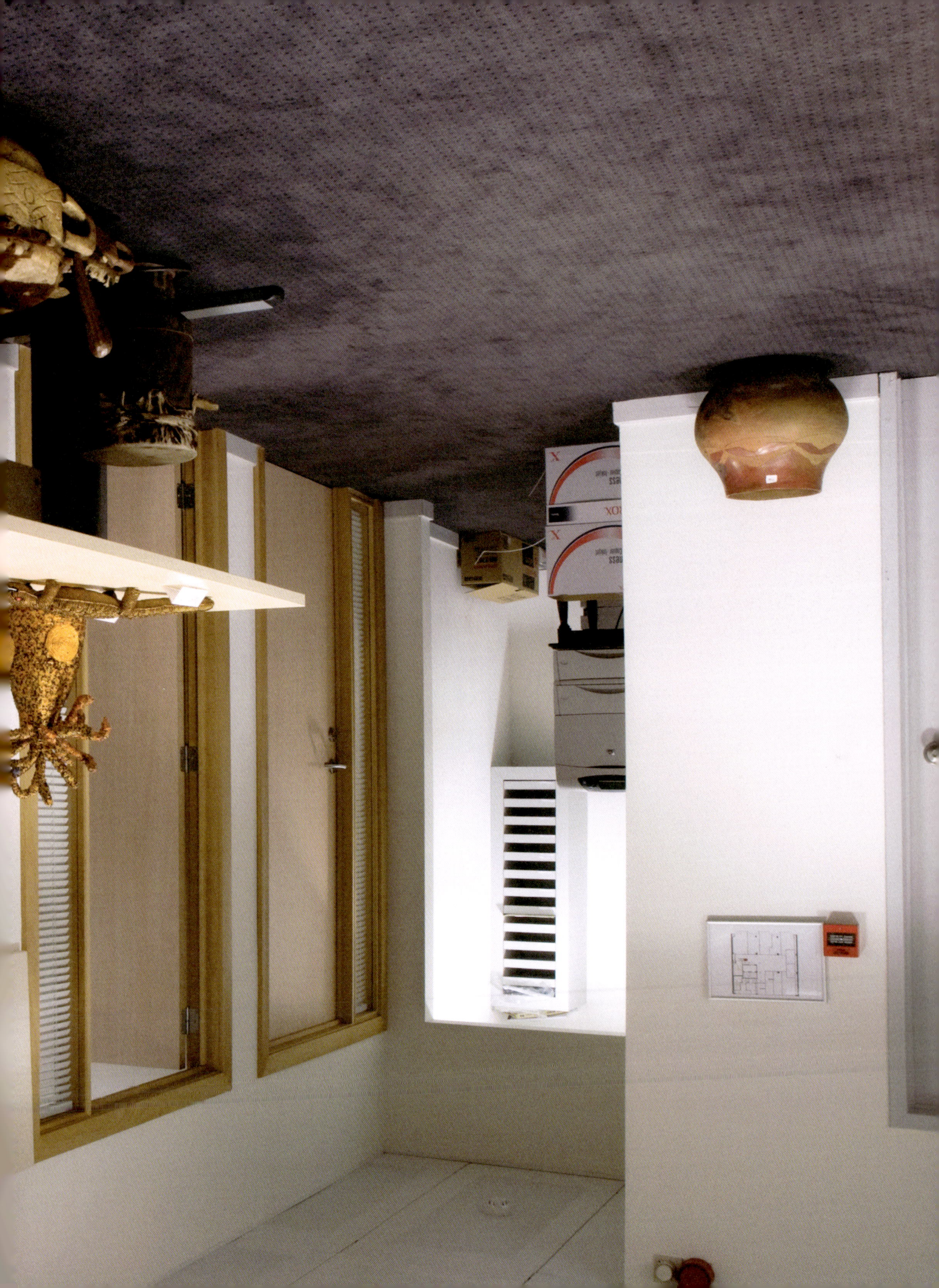

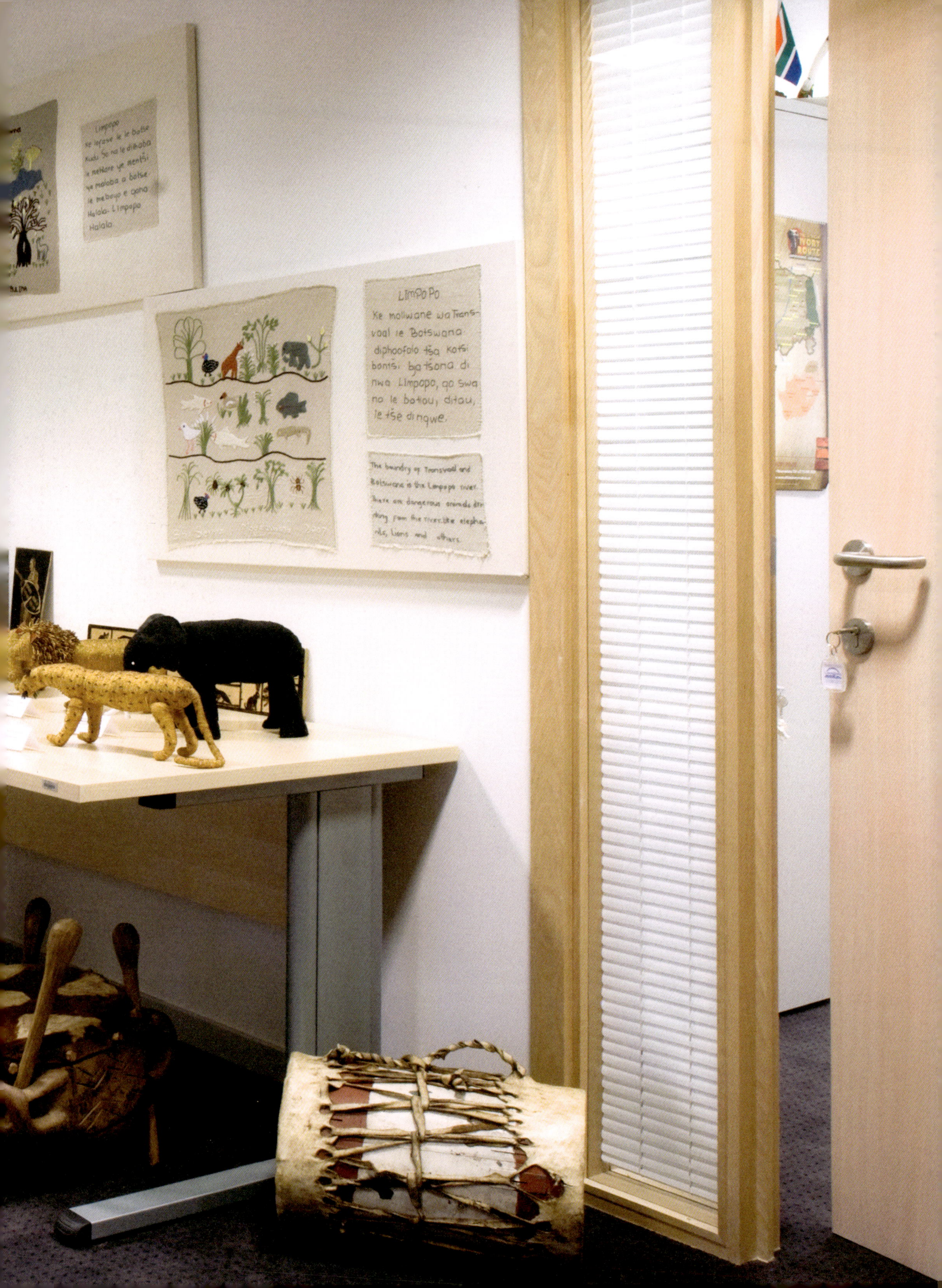
Limpopo
Ke moliwane wa Trans-
vaal le Botswana
diphoofolo tša kotsi
bontši bja tšona di
nwa Limpopo, go swa
no le botou, ditau,
le tše dingwe.
The boundry of Transvaal and
Botswana is the Limpopo river.
There are dangerous animals drin-
king from the river like elepha-
nts, lions and others.

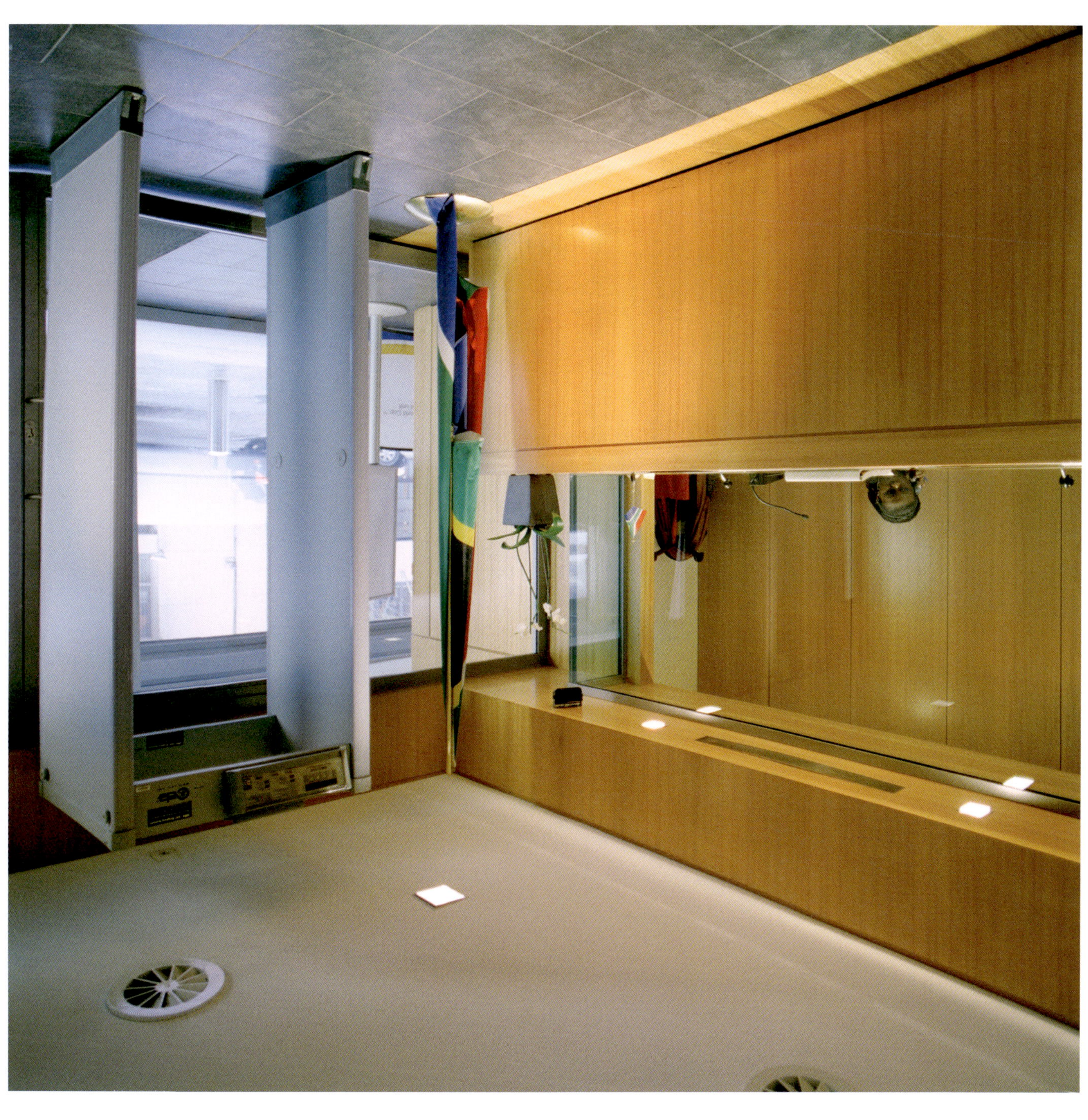

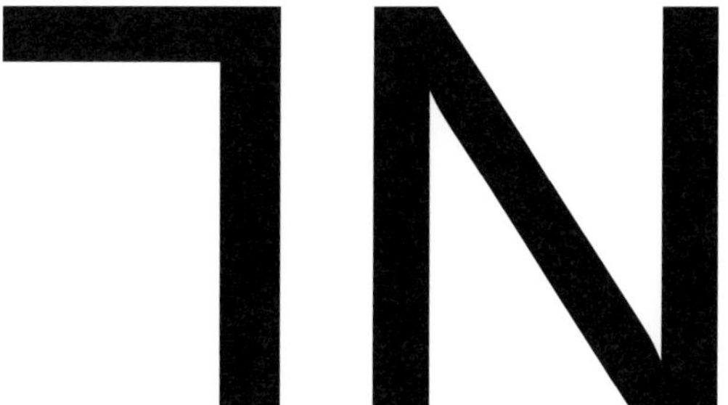

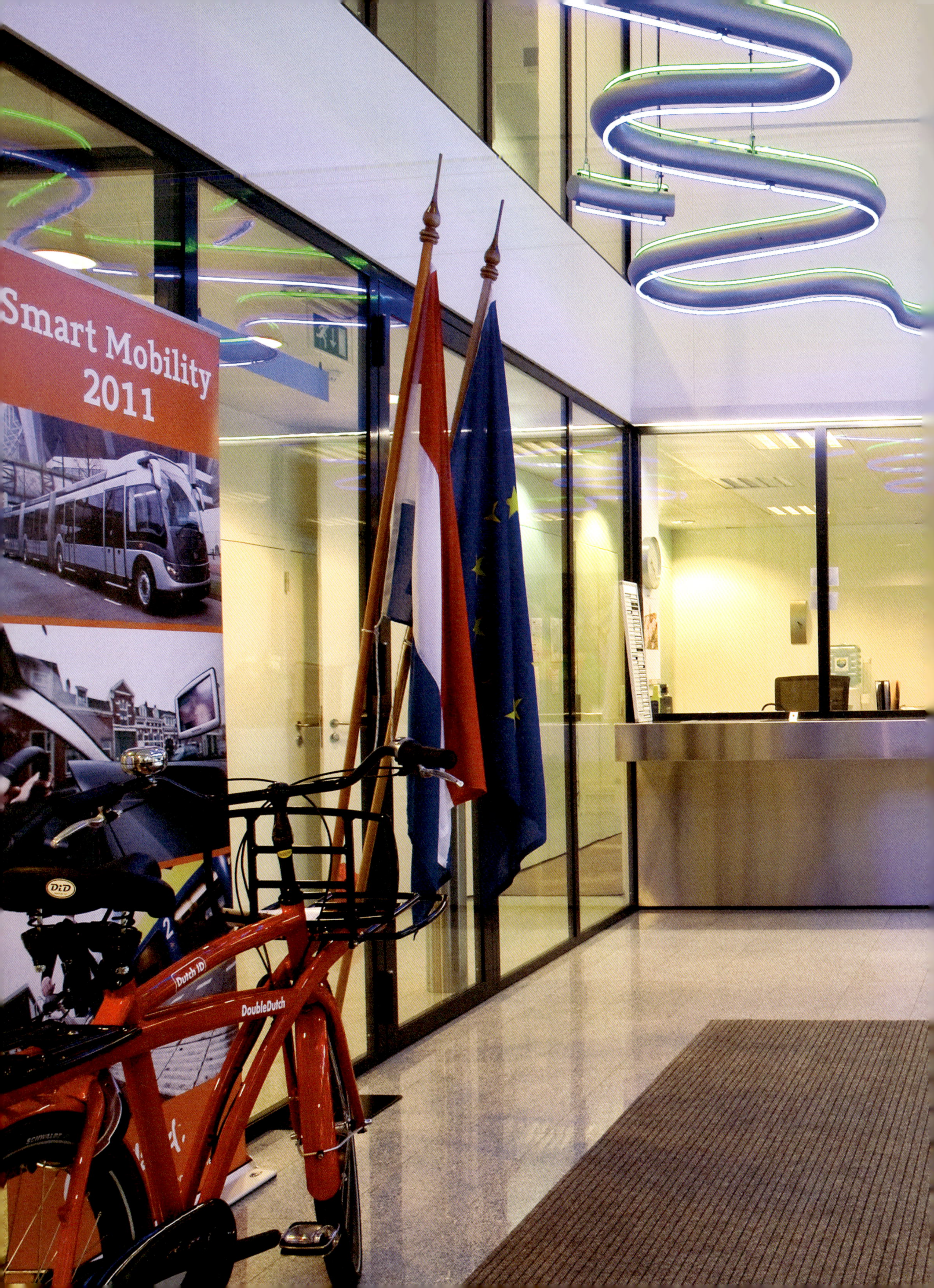
Smart Mobility
2011
DoubleDutch
Dutch ID

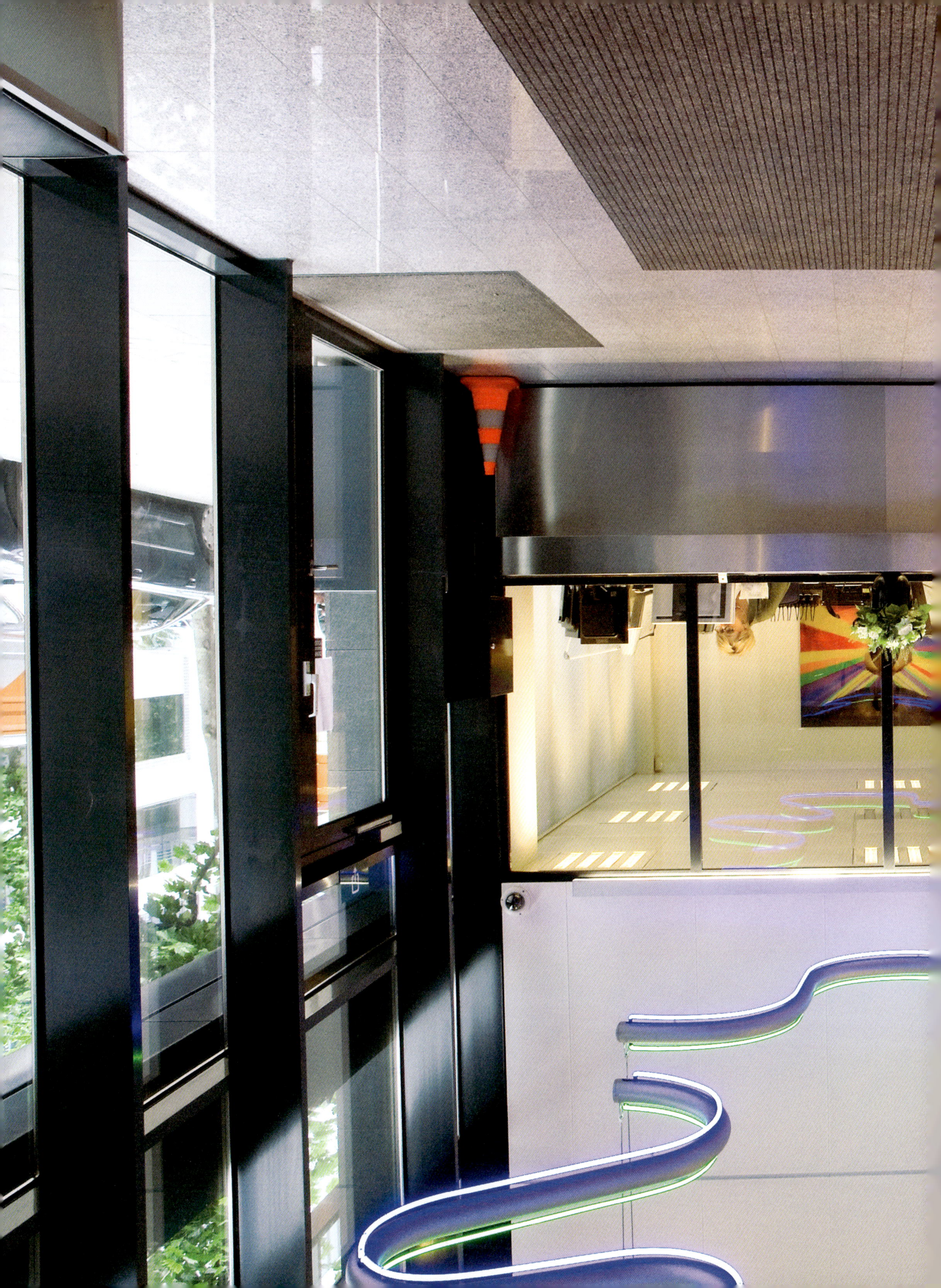

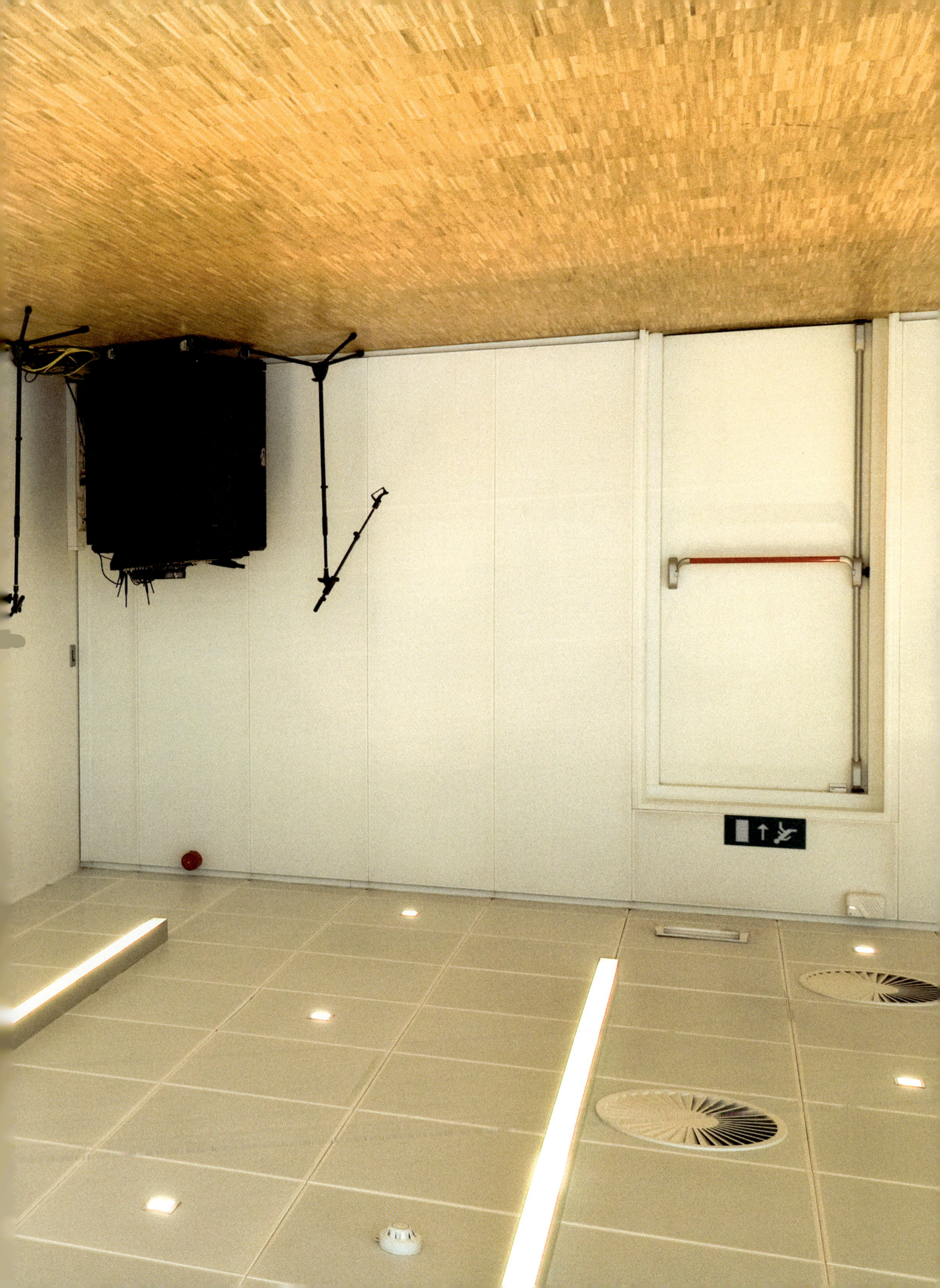

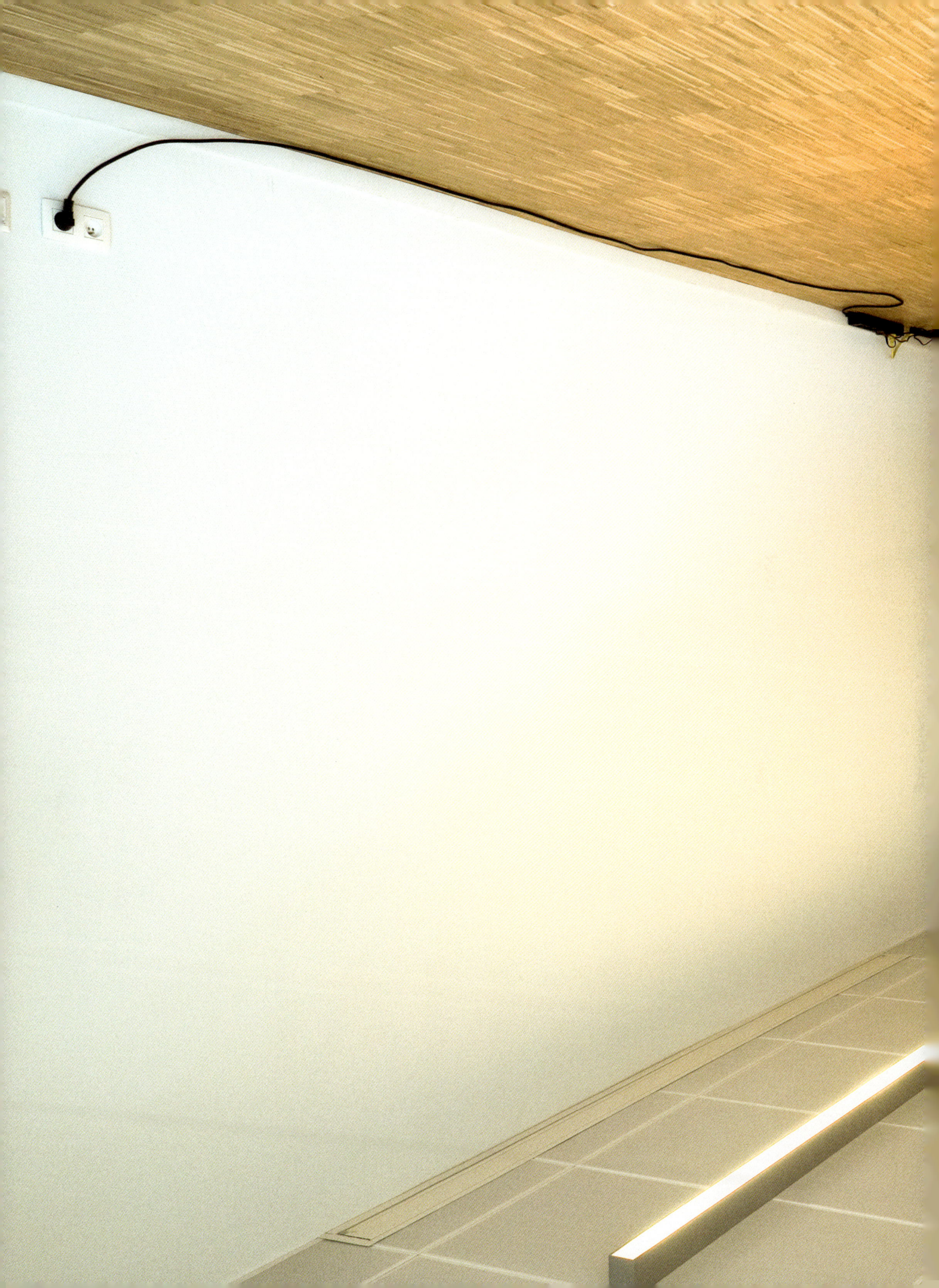

MN

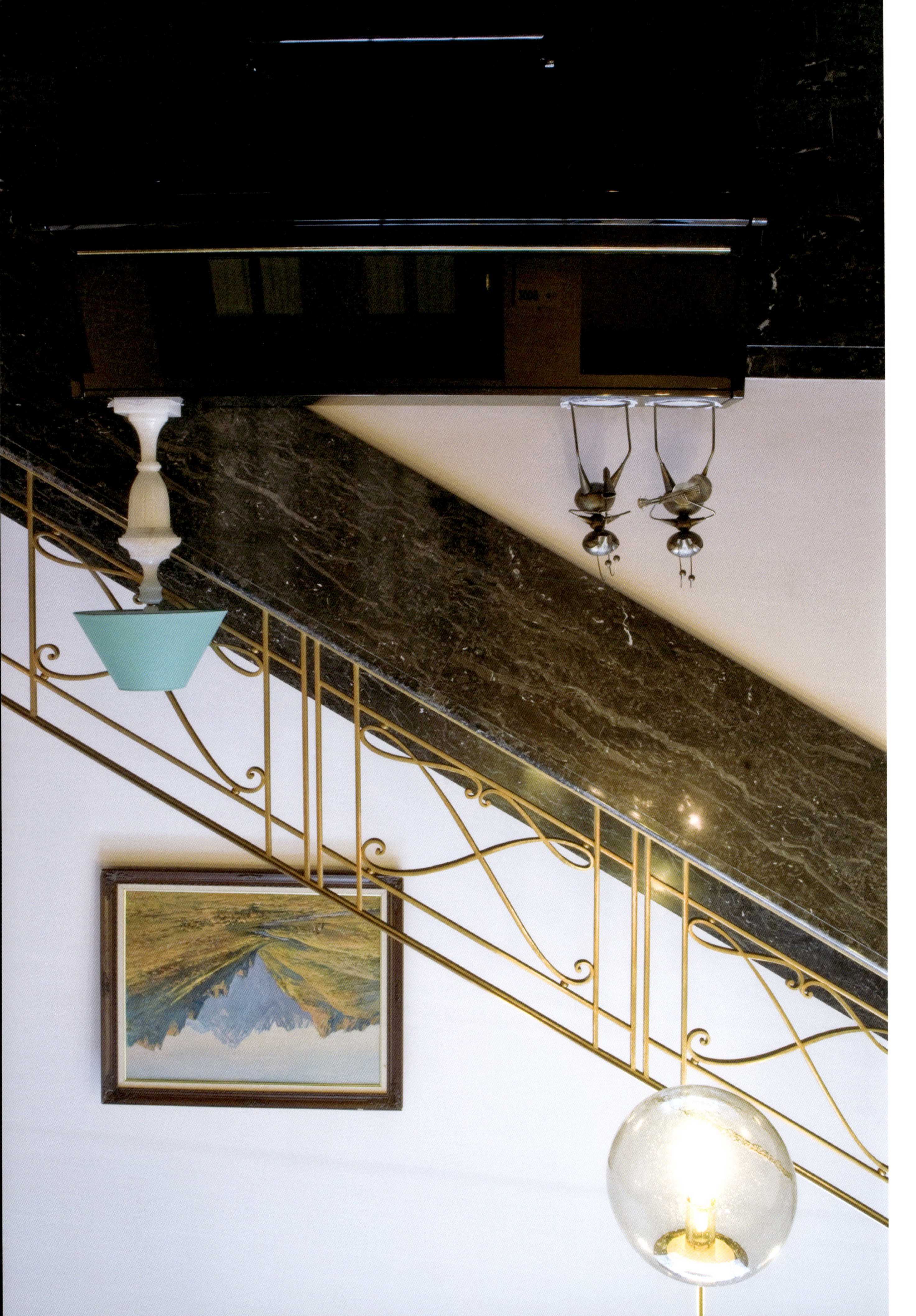

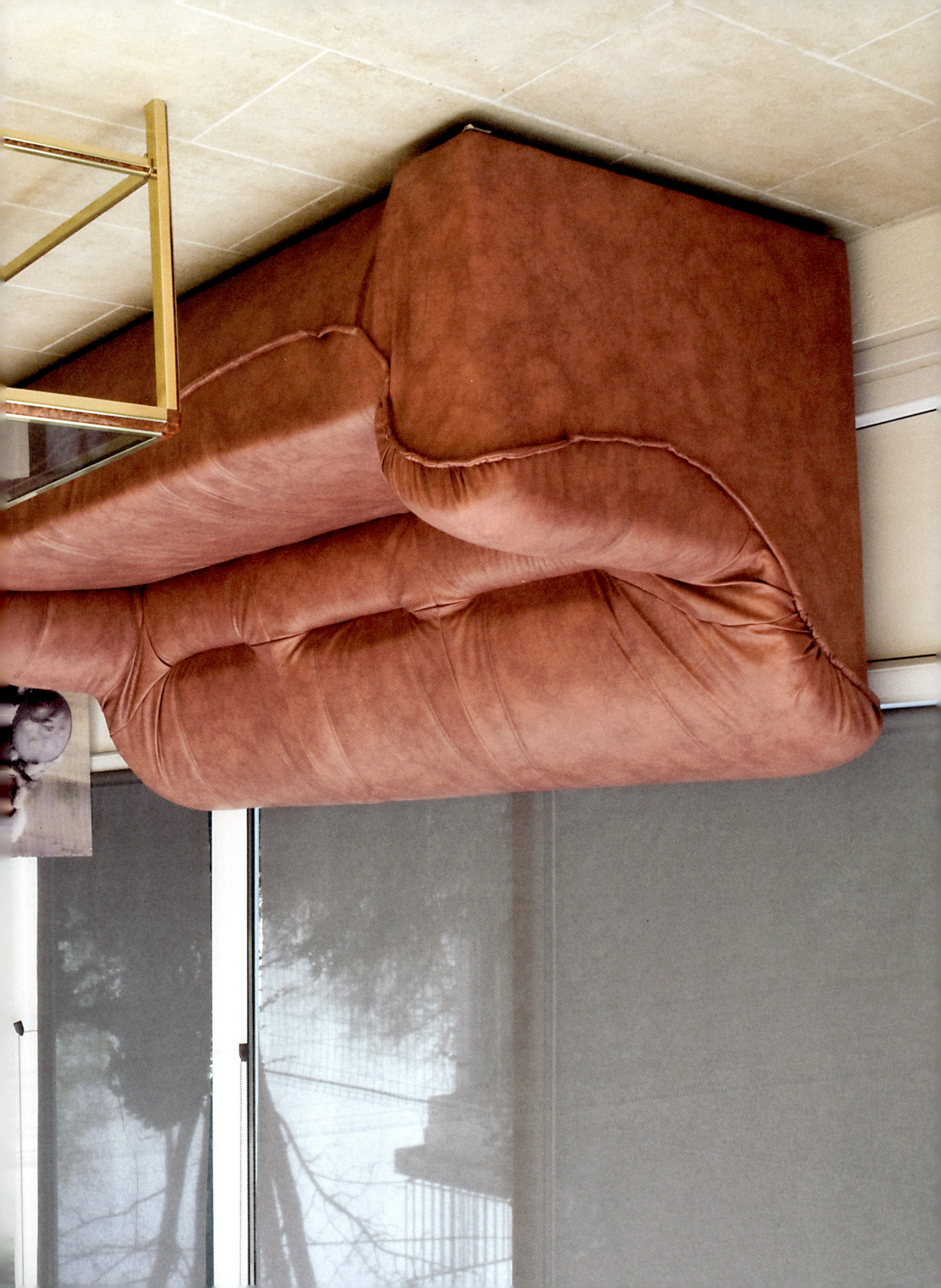

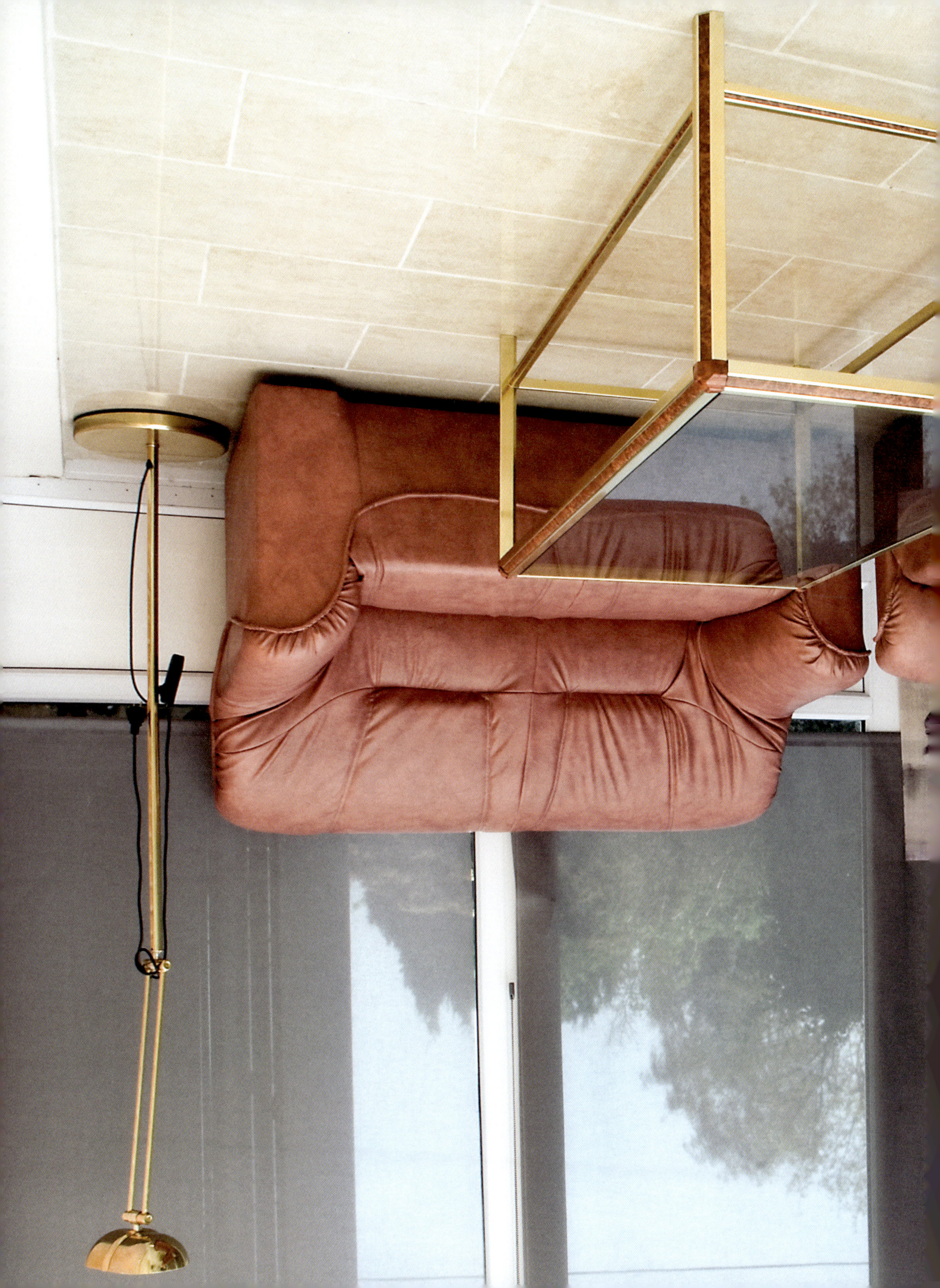

AD

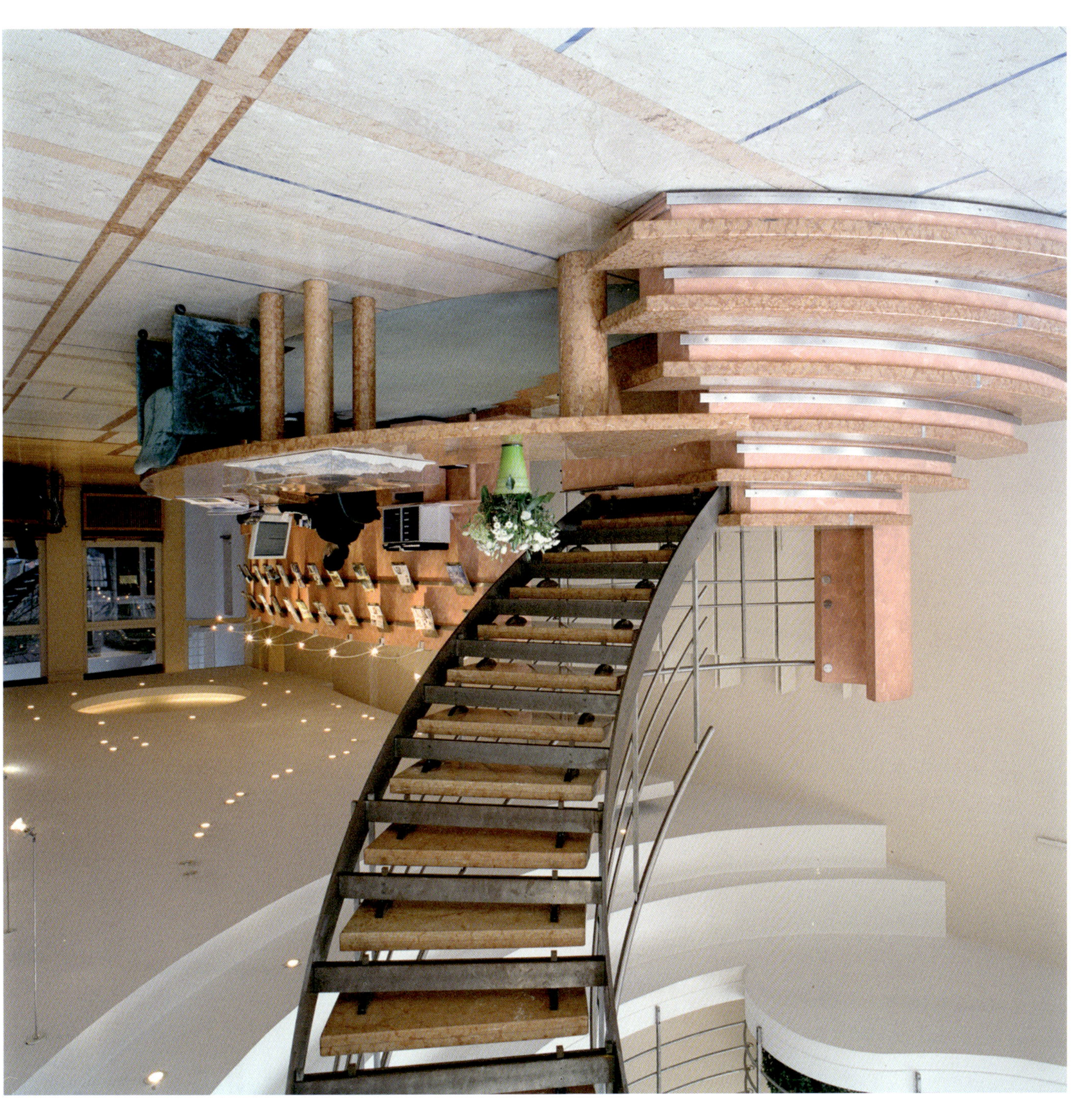

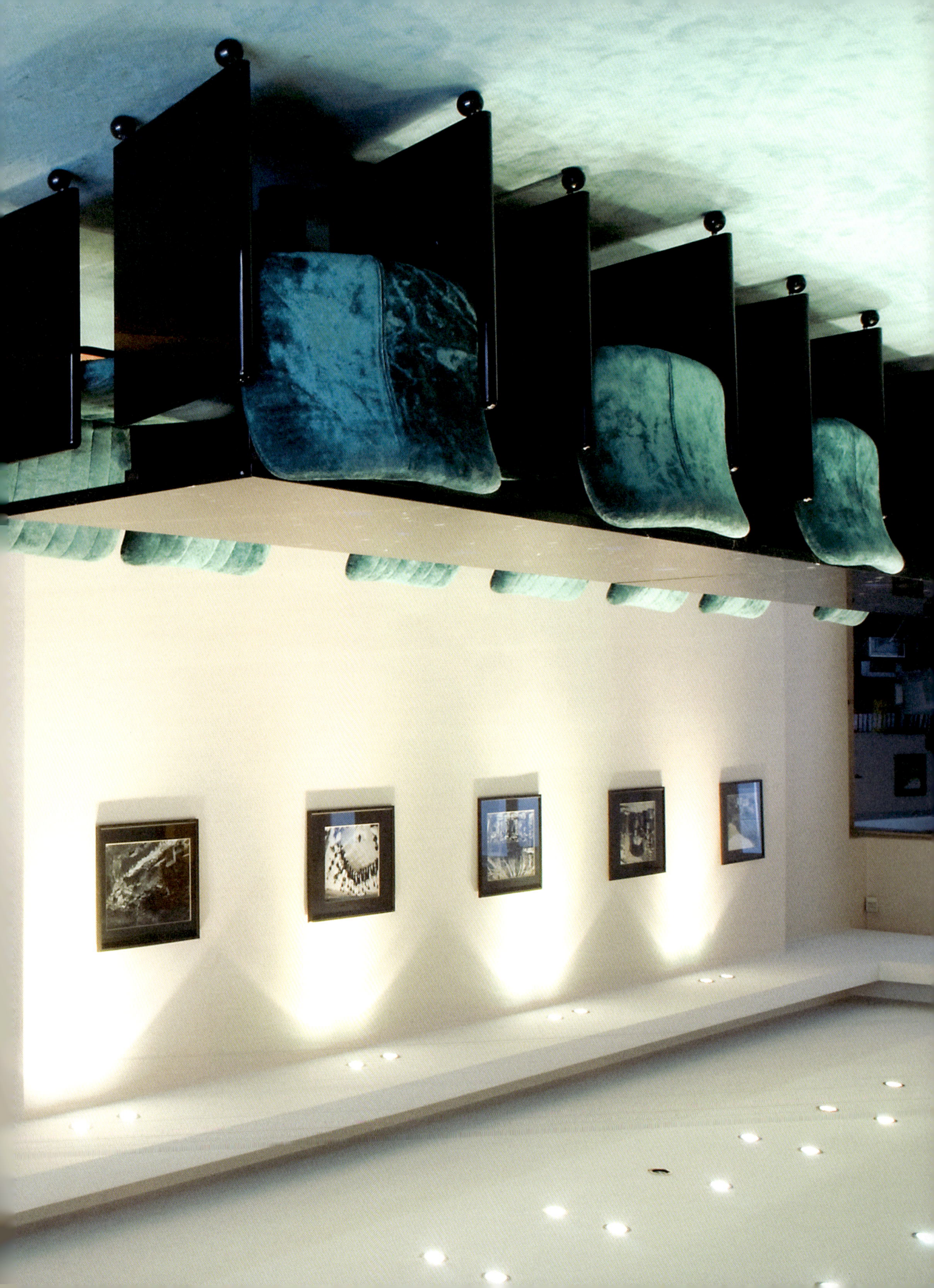

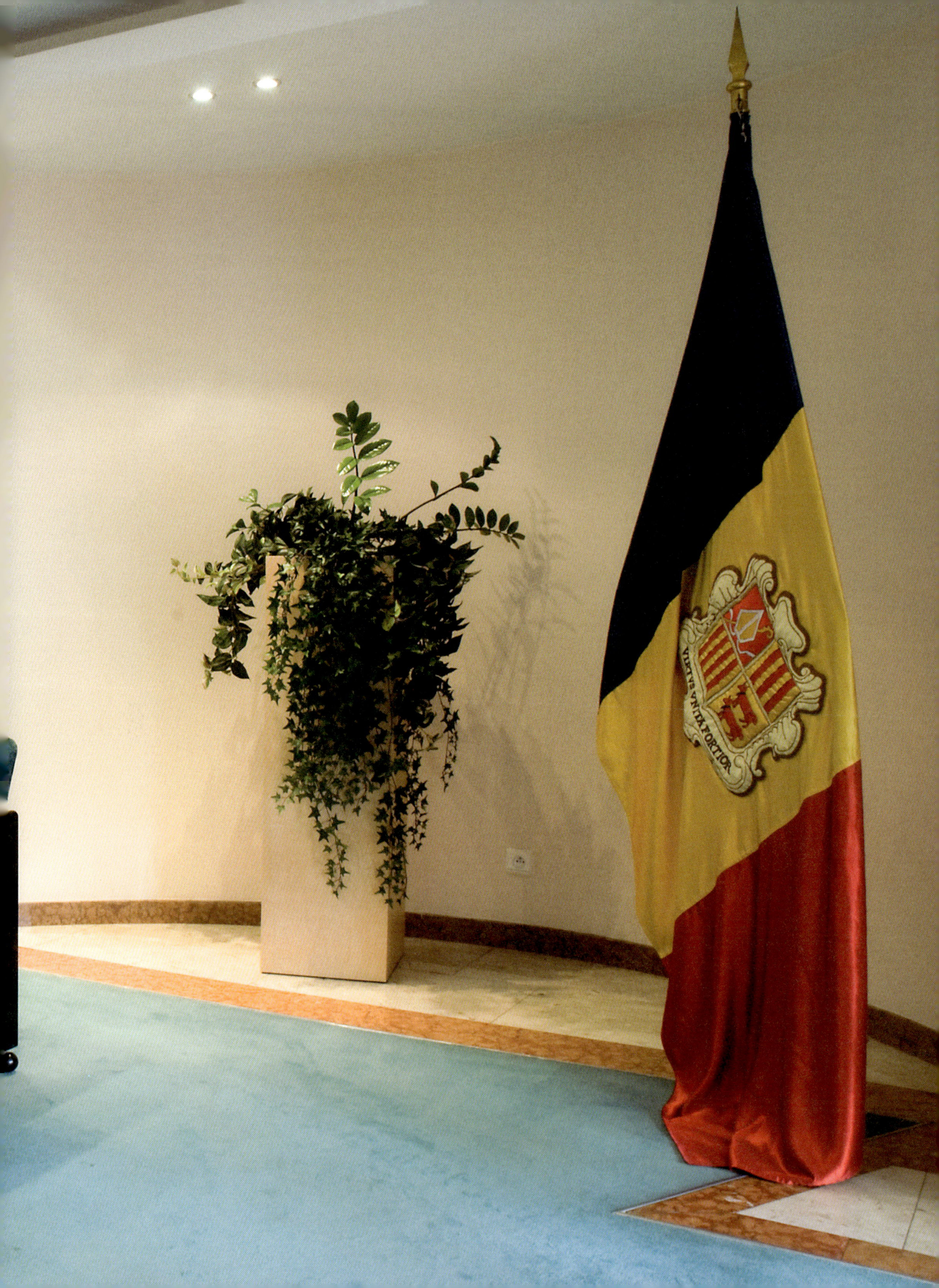
VIRTVS VNITA FORTIOR

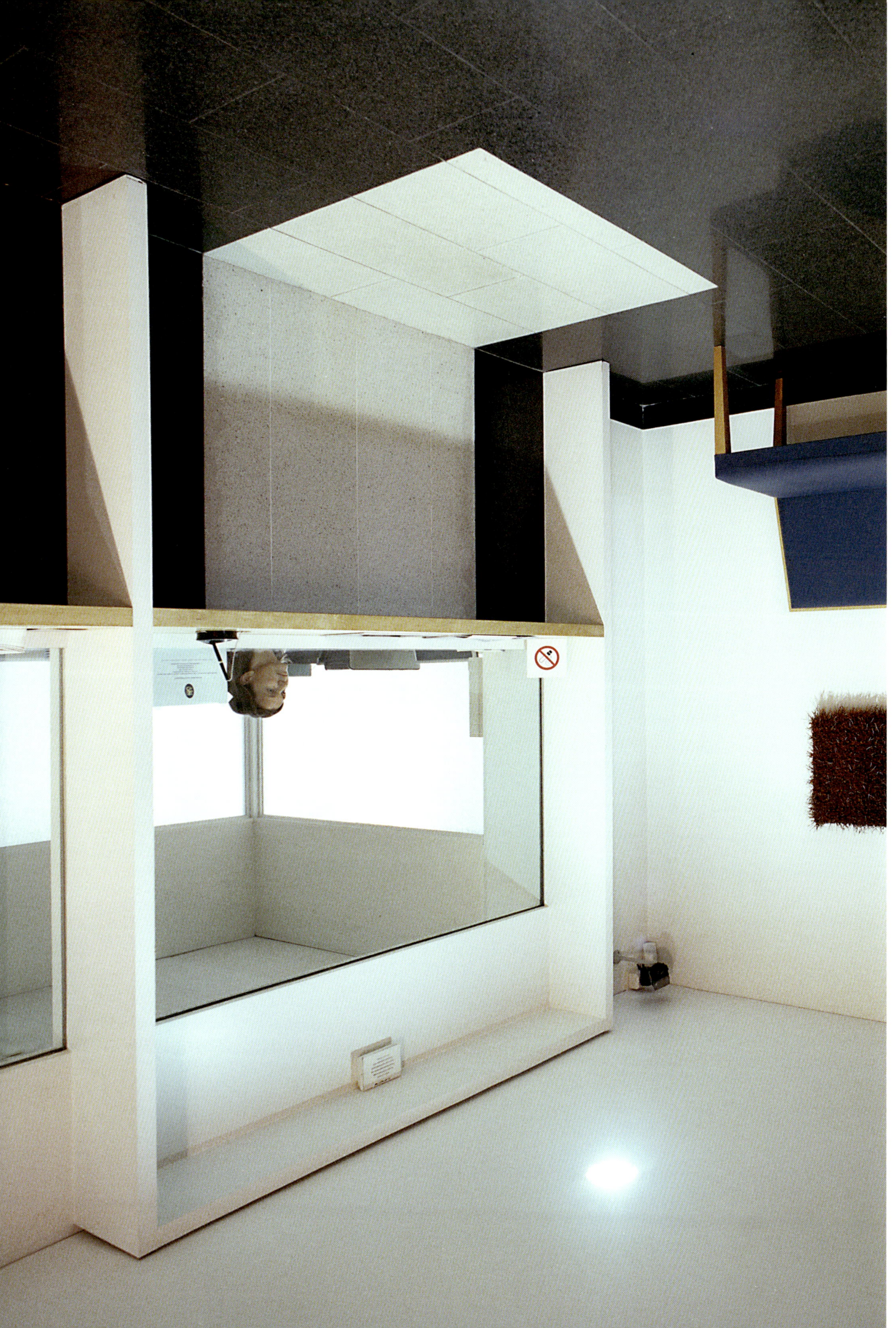

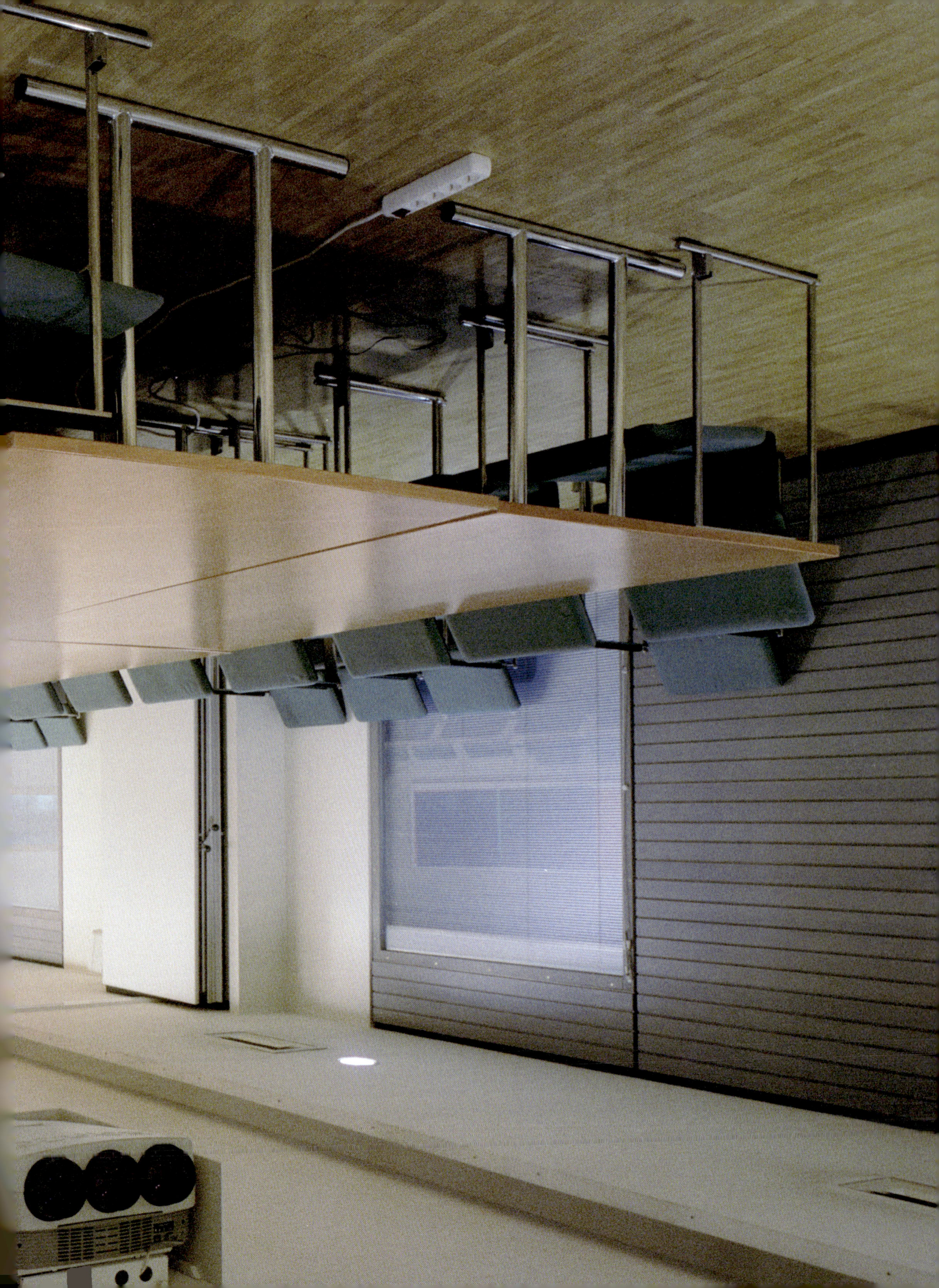

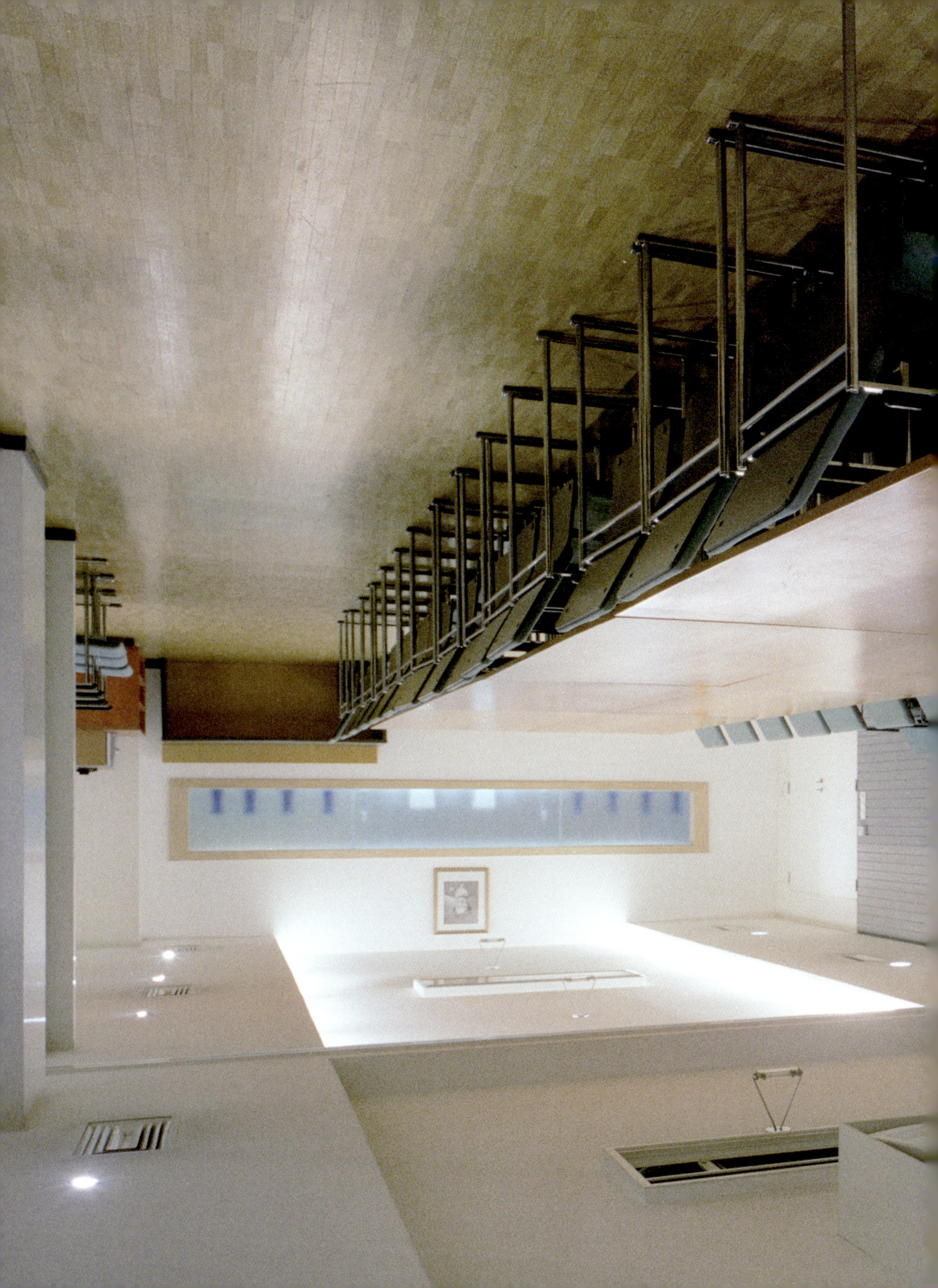

SI

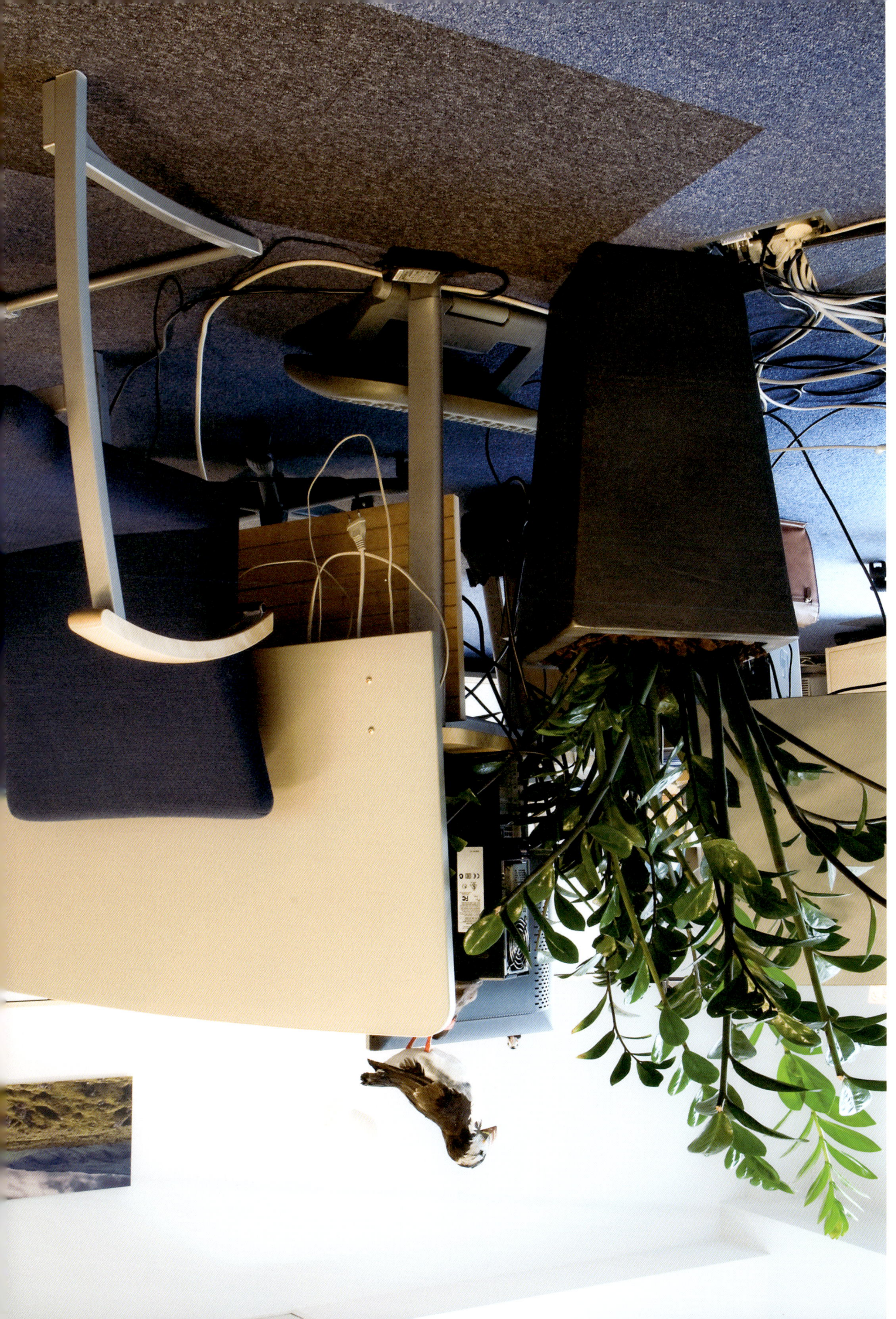

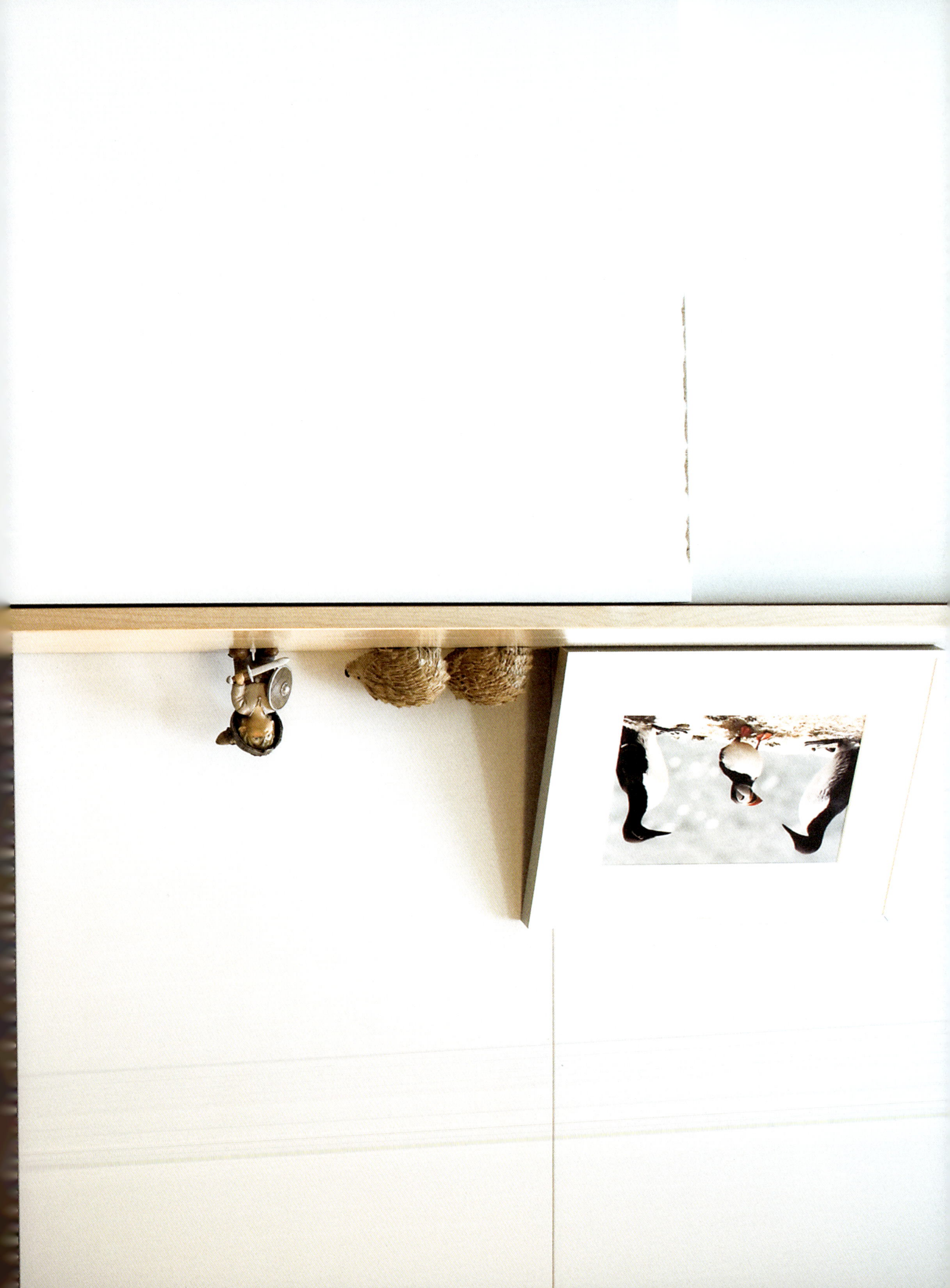

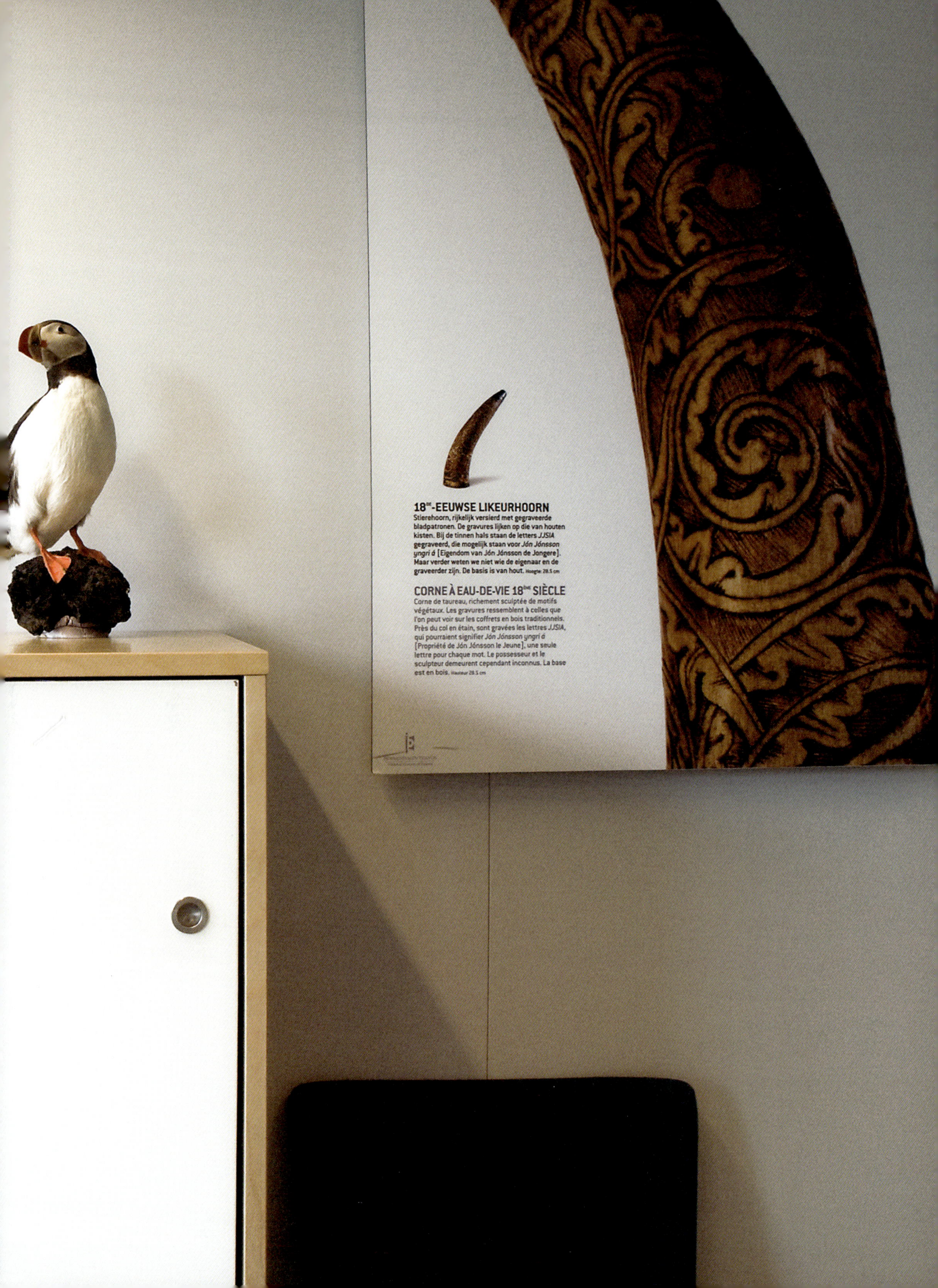
18ᴱ-EEUWSE LIKEURHOORN
Stierehoorn, rijkelijk versierd met gegraveerde bladpatronen. De gravures lijken op die van houten kisten. Bij de tinnen hals staan de letters *JJSIA* gegraveerd, die mogelijk staan voor *Jón Jónsson yngri á* [Eigendom van Jón Jónsson de Jongere]. Maar verder weten we niet wie de eigenaar en de graveerder zijn. De basis is van hout. Hoogte: 28.5 cm
CORNE À EAU-DE-VIE 18ᴱ SIÈCLE
Corne de taureau, richement sculptée de motifs végétaux. Les gravures ressemblent à celles que l'on peut voir sur les coffrets en bois traditionnels. Près du col en étain, sont gravées les lettres *JJSIA*, qui pourraient signifier *Jón Jónsson yngri á* [Propriété de Jón Jónsson le Jeune], une seule lettre pour chaque mot. Le possesseur et le sculpteur demeurent cependant inconnus. La base est en bois. Hauteur 28.5 cm

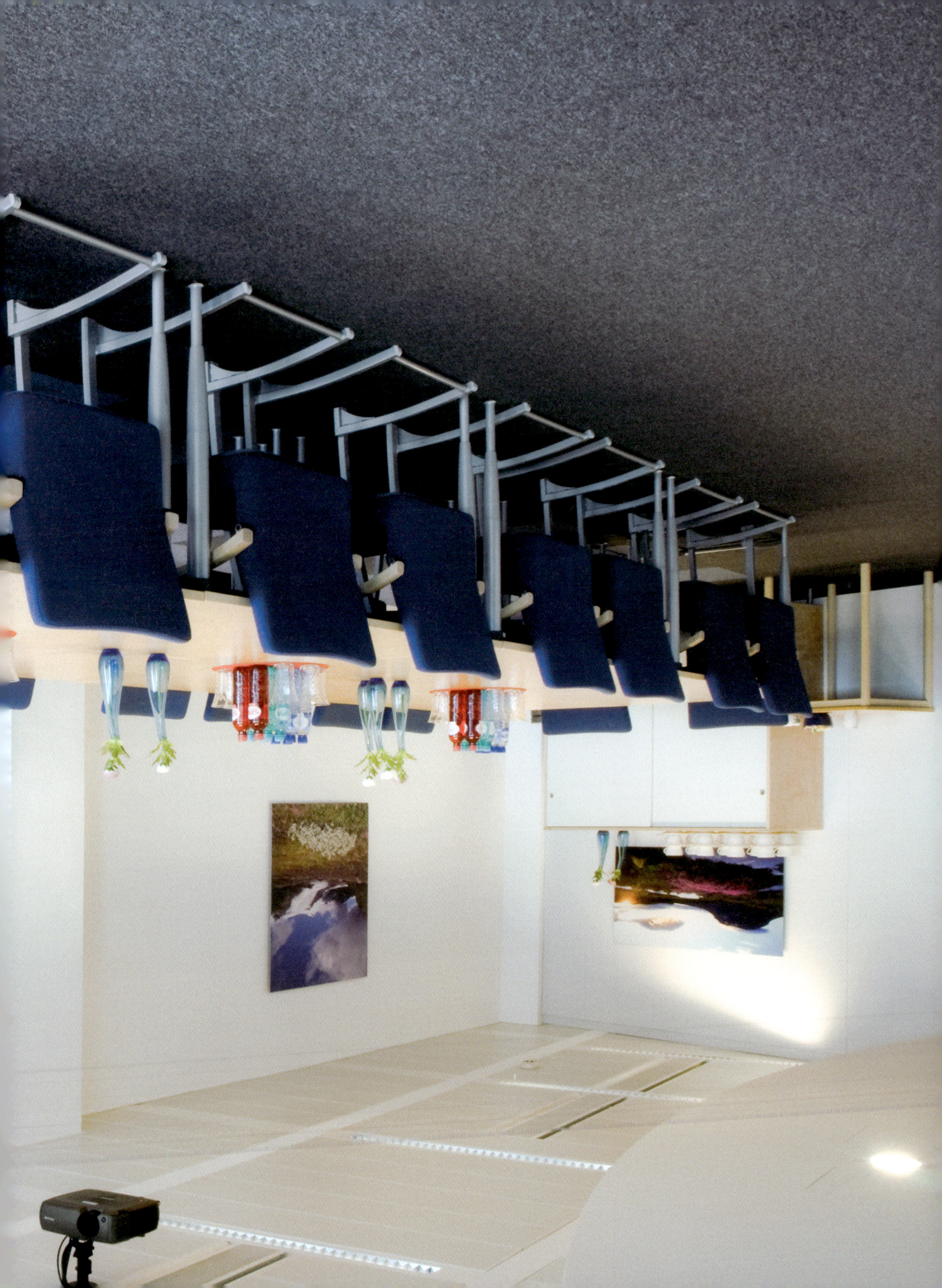

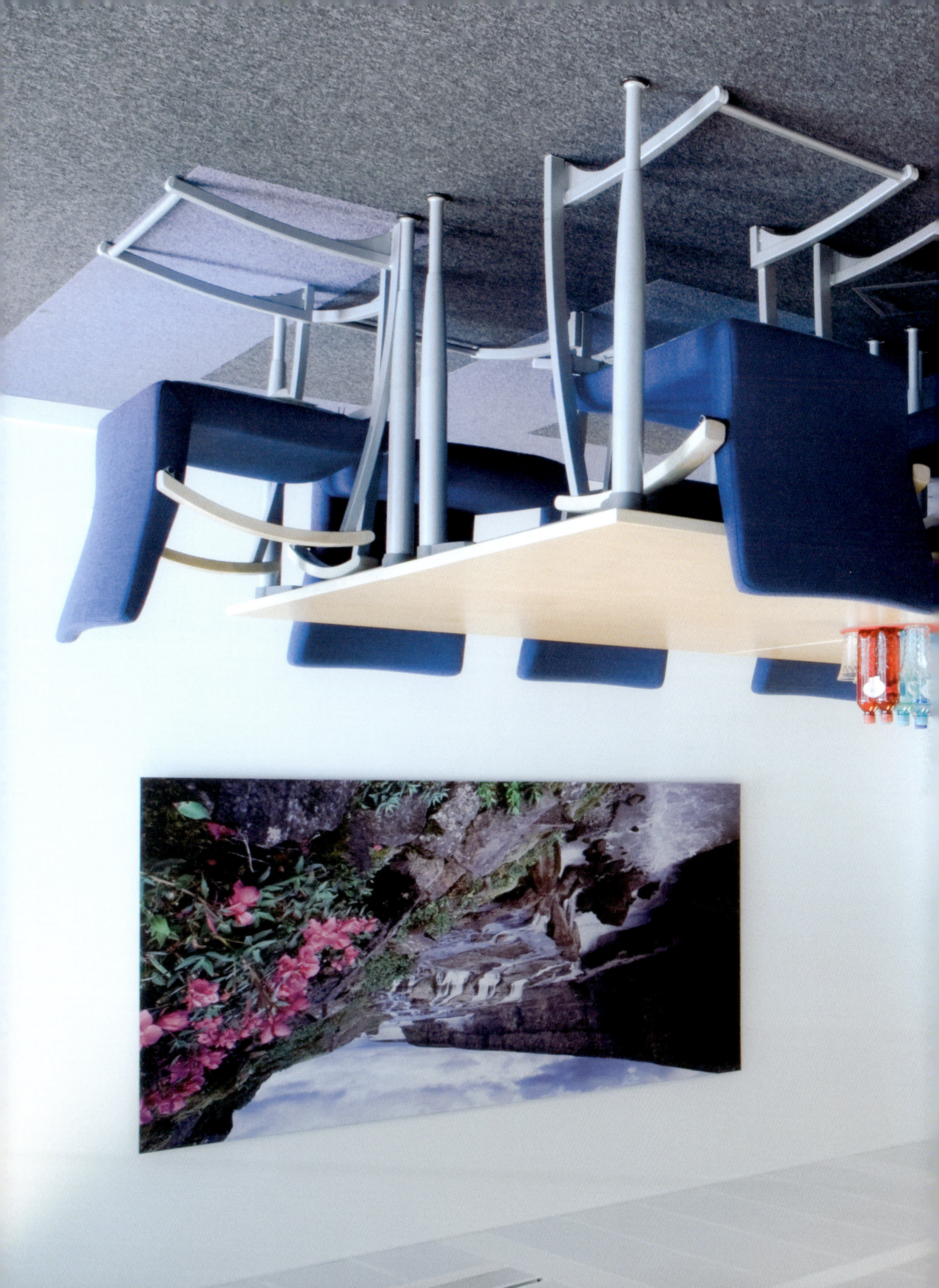

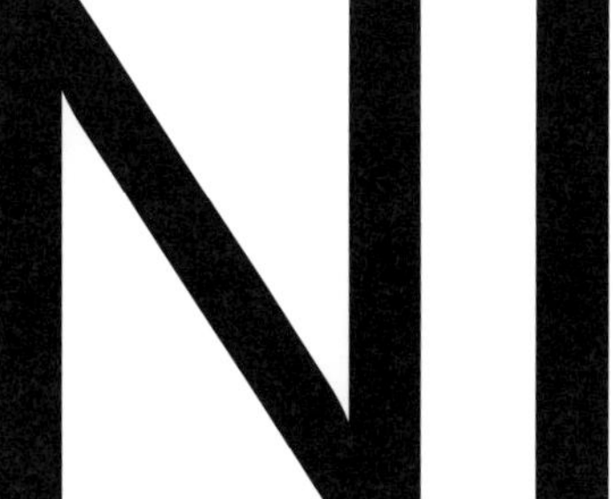
NI

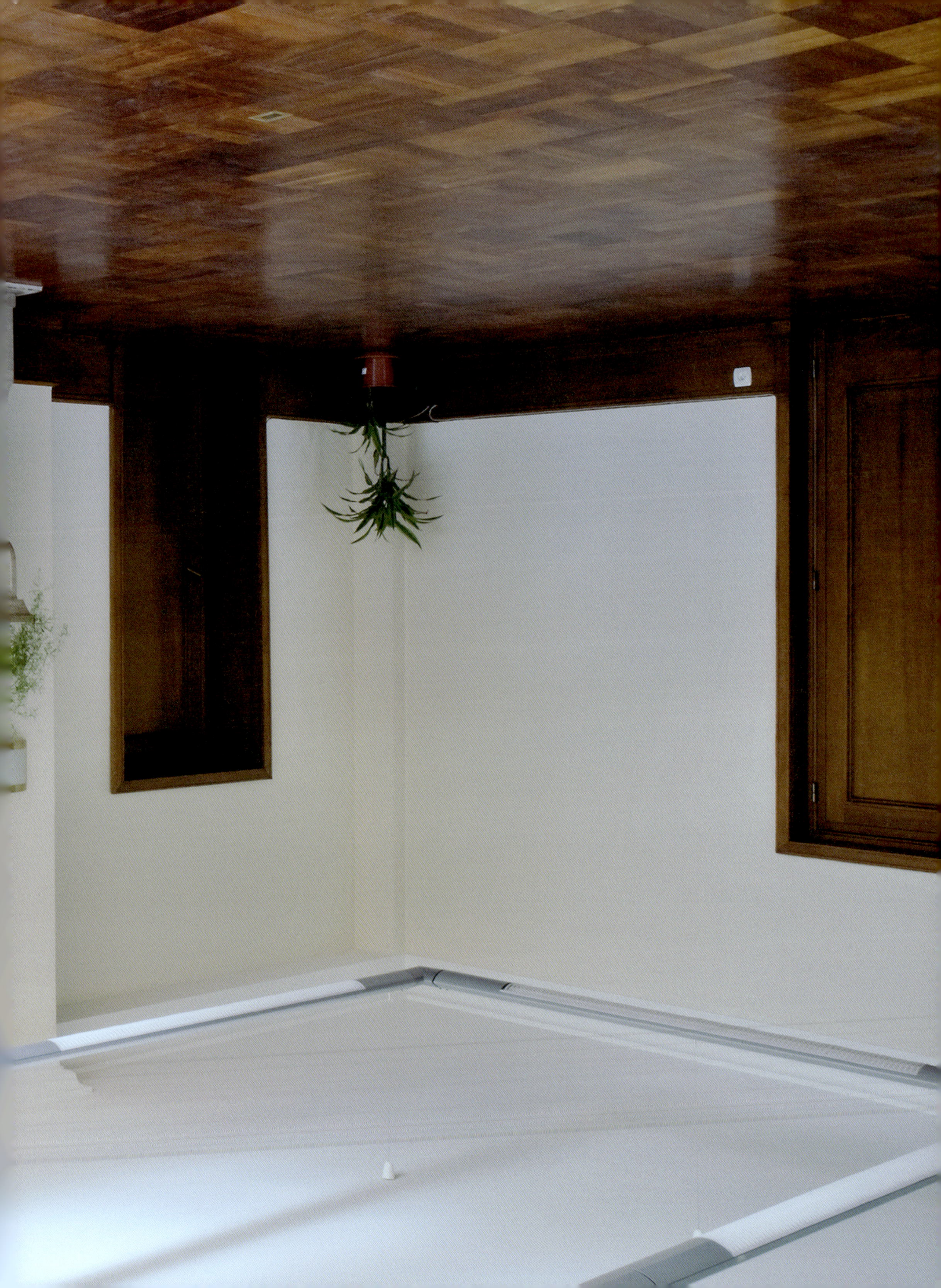

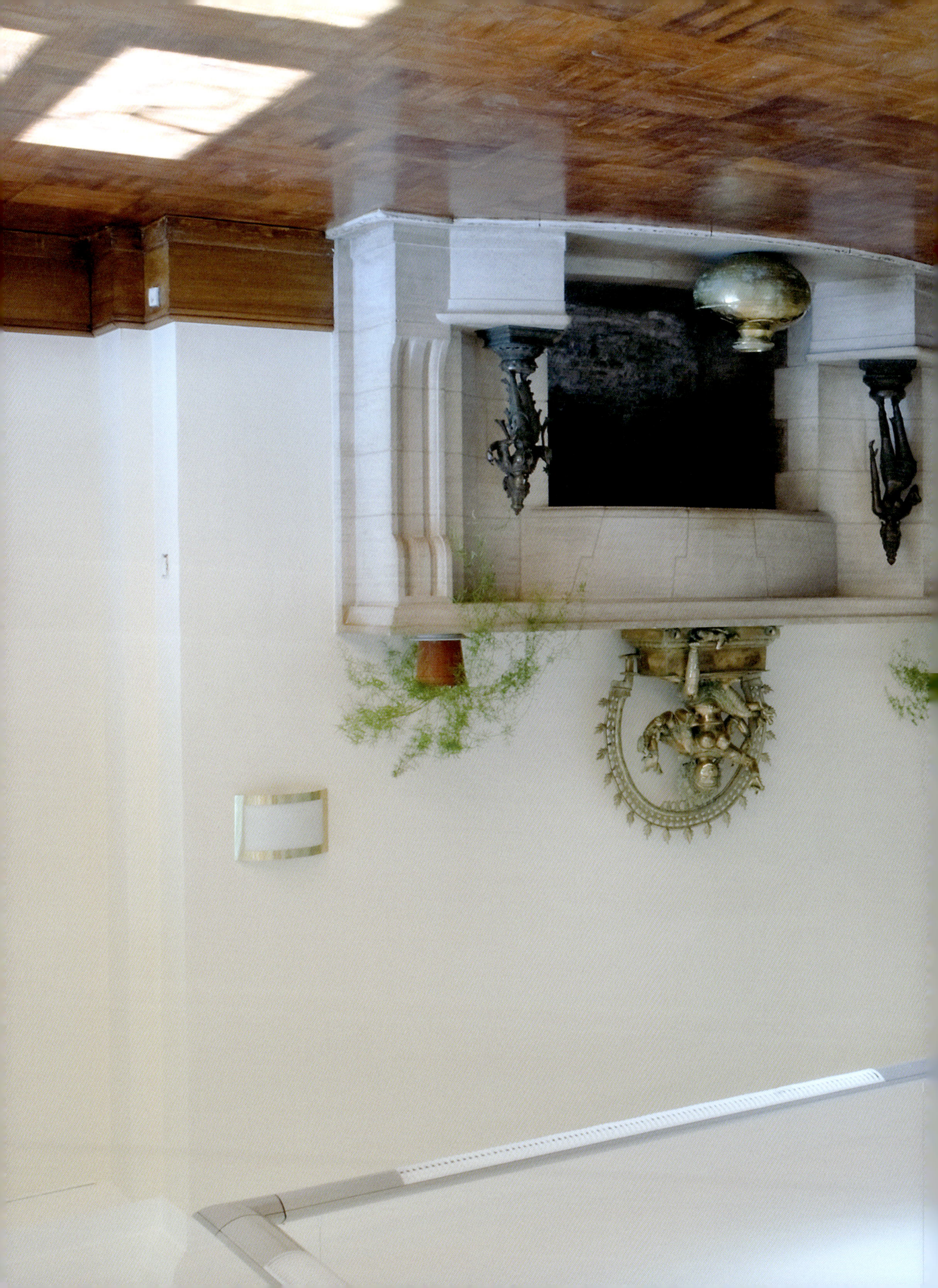

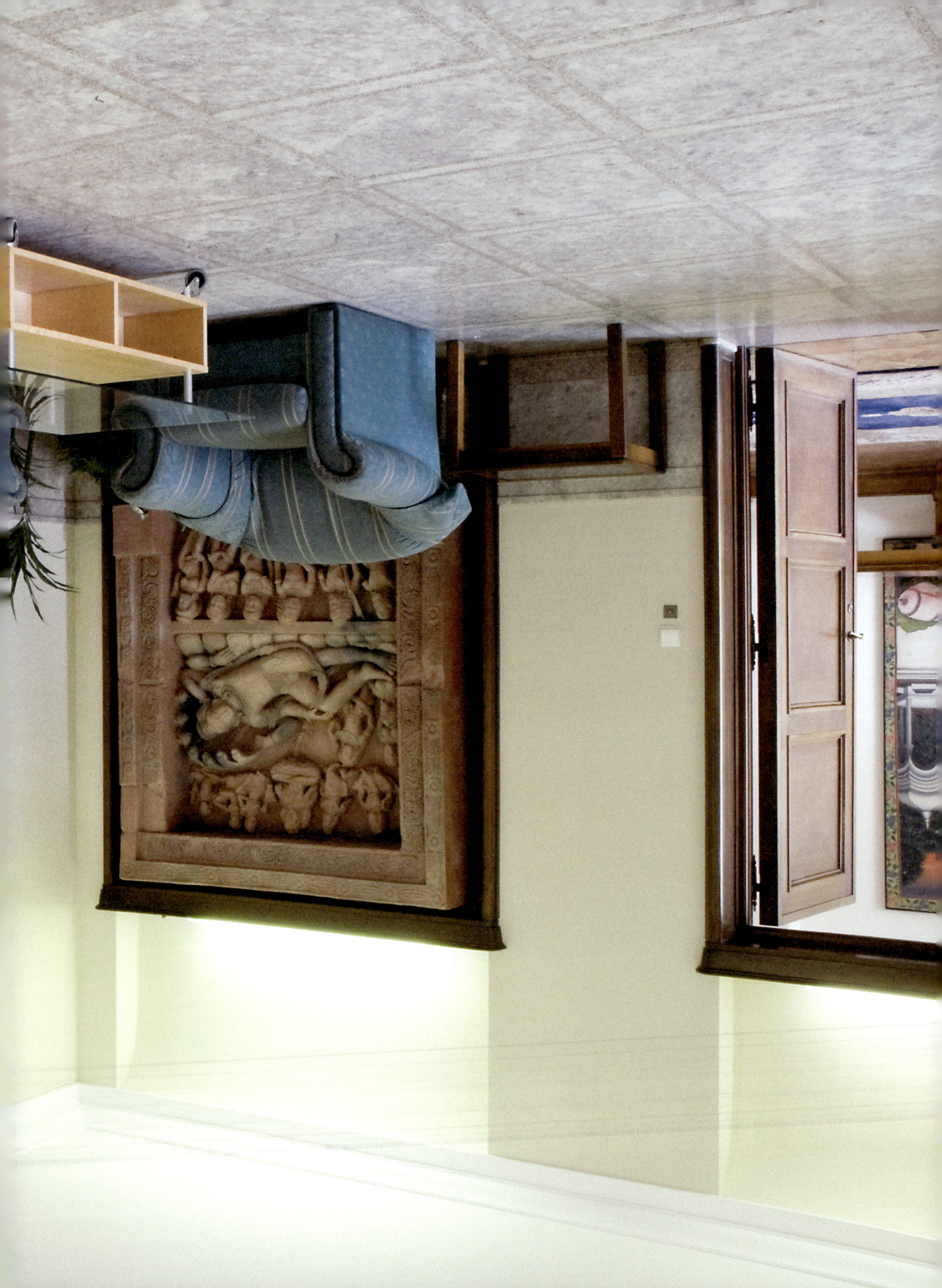

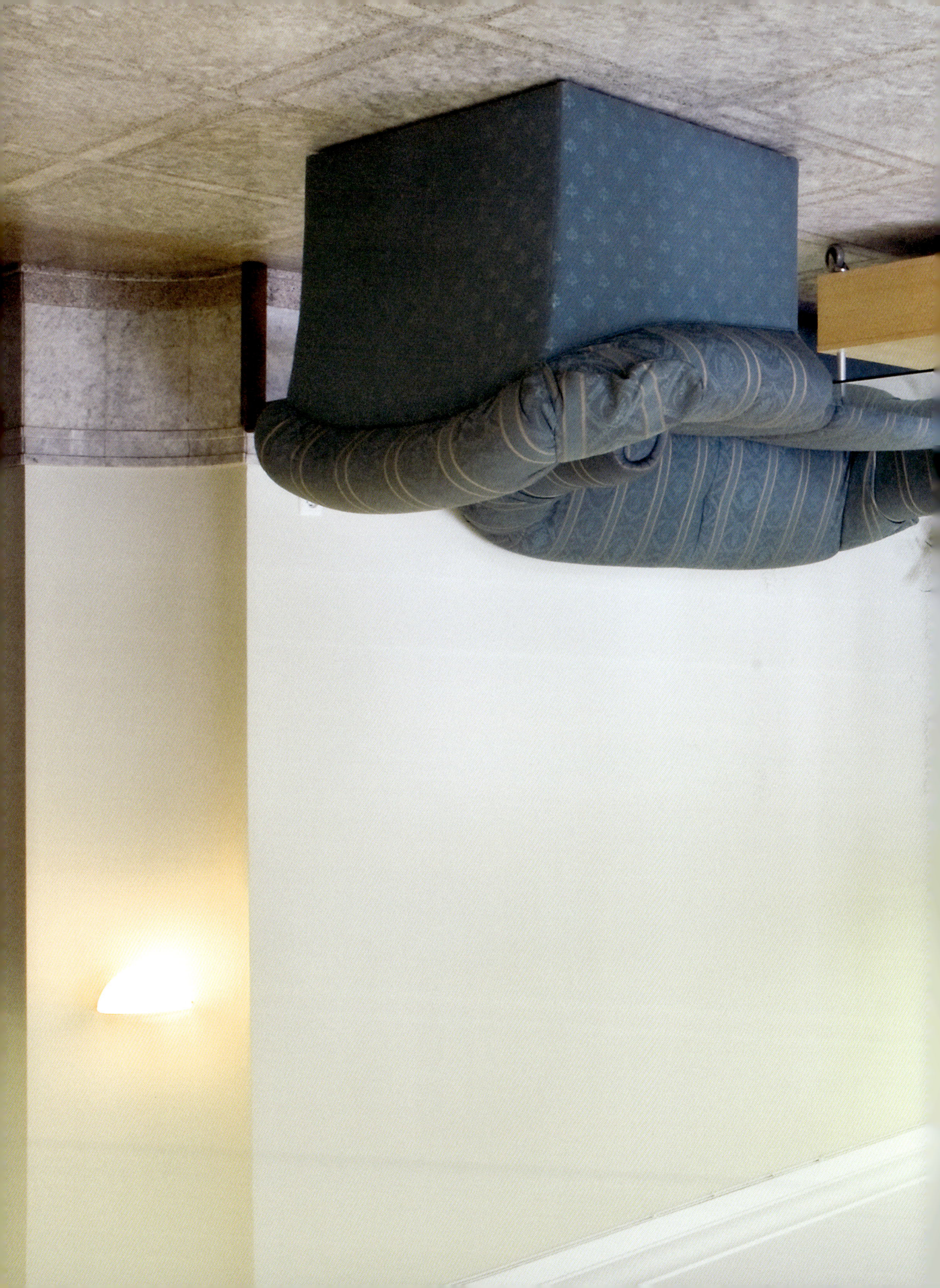

ID

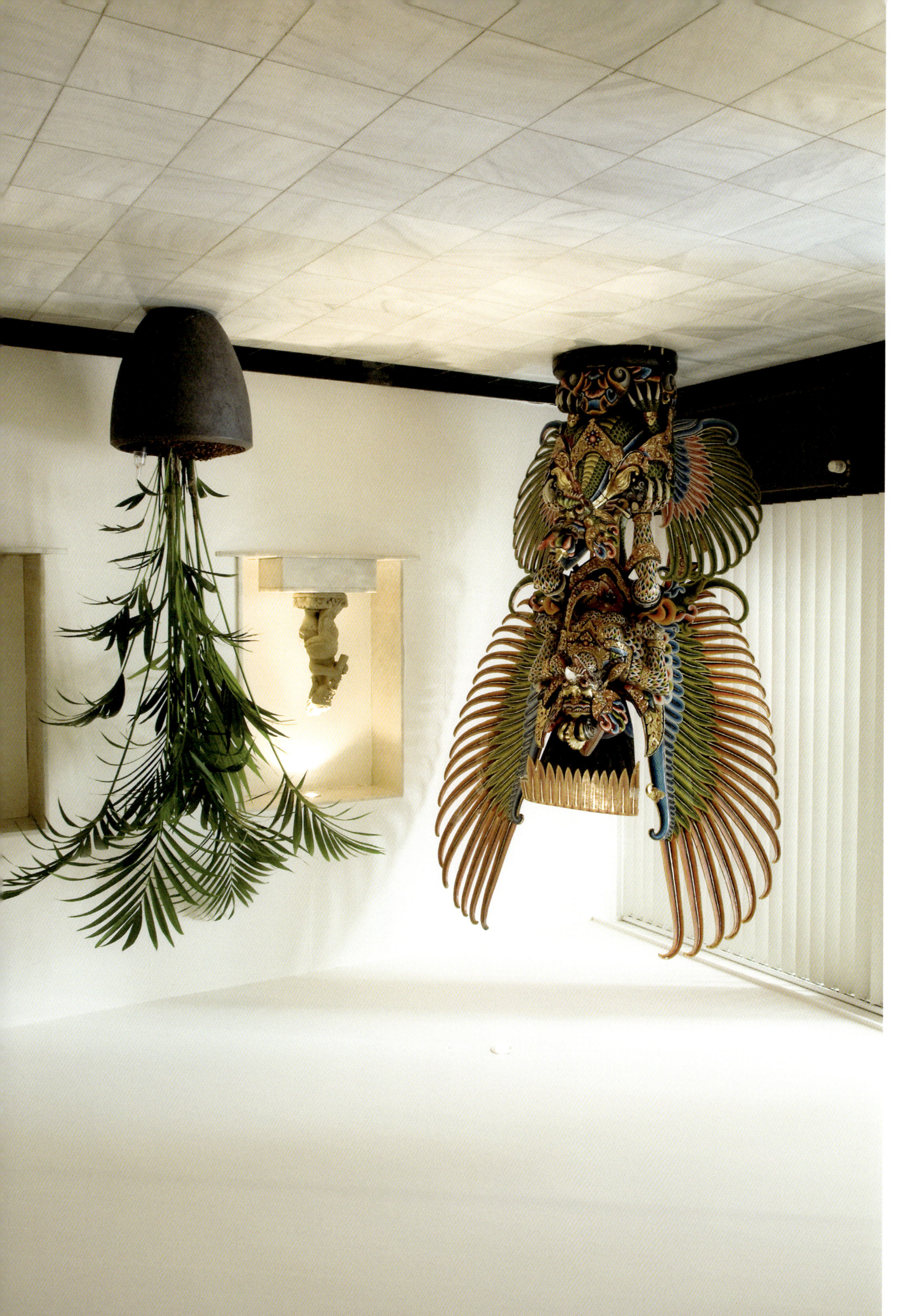

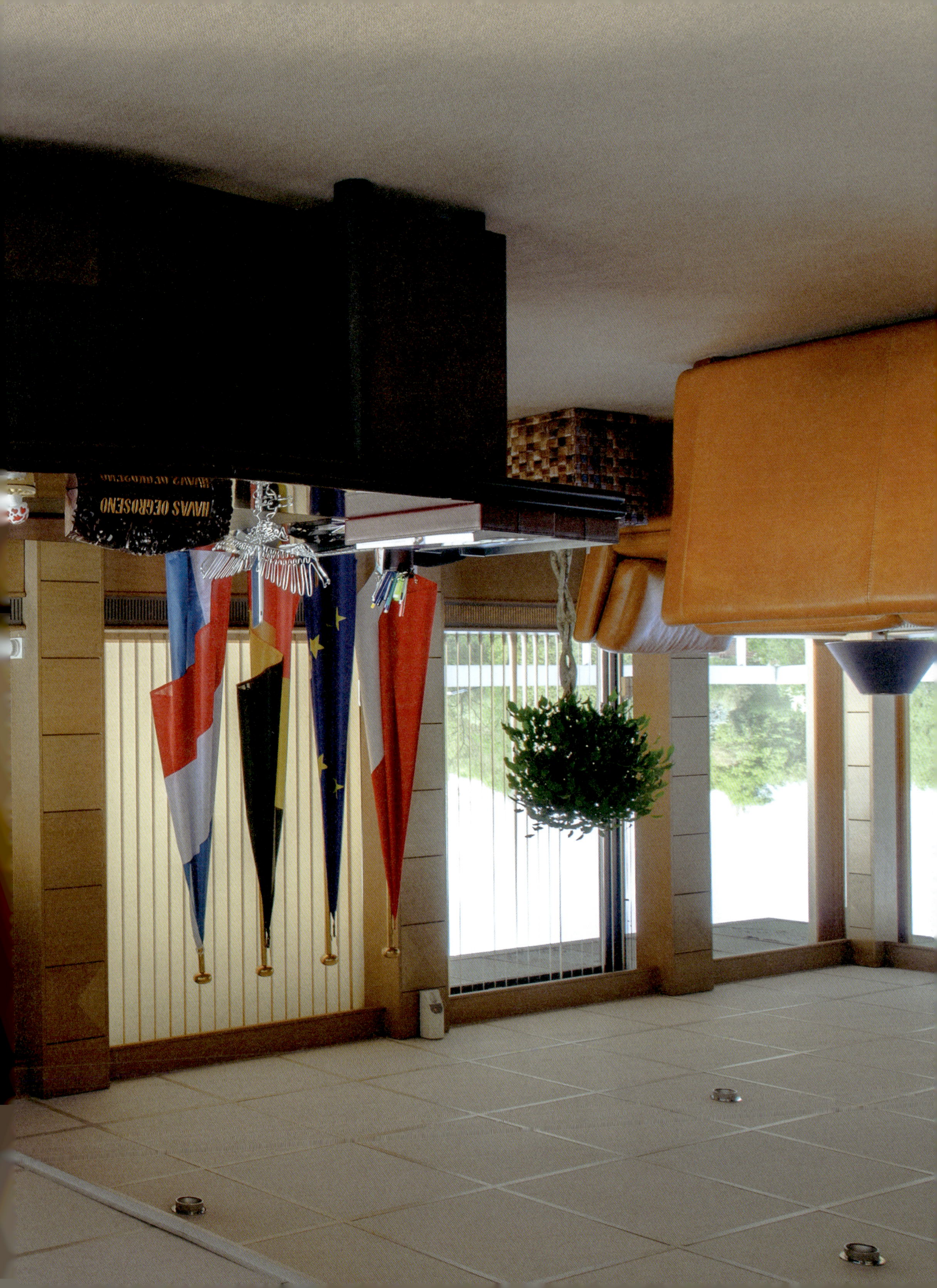

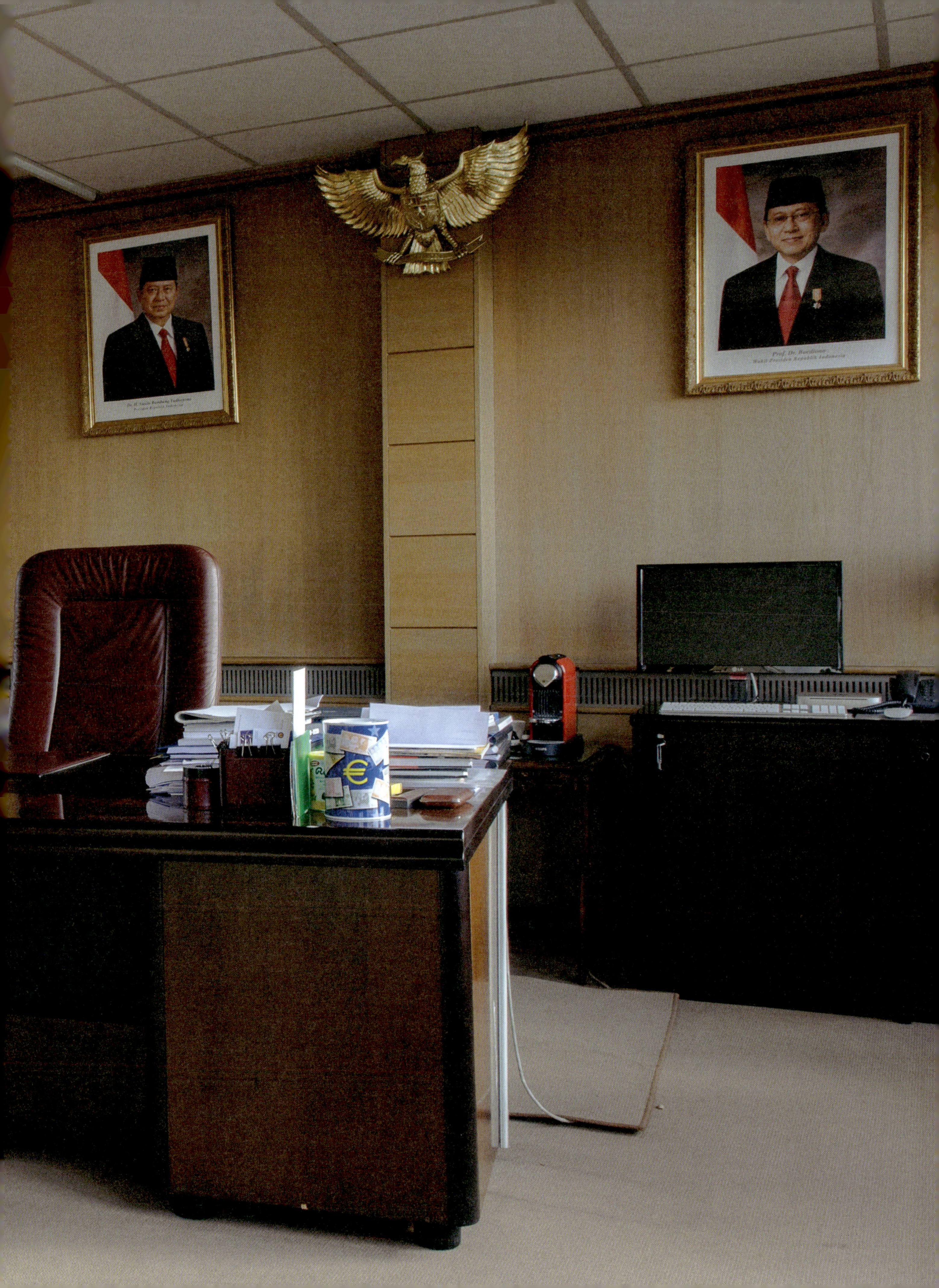

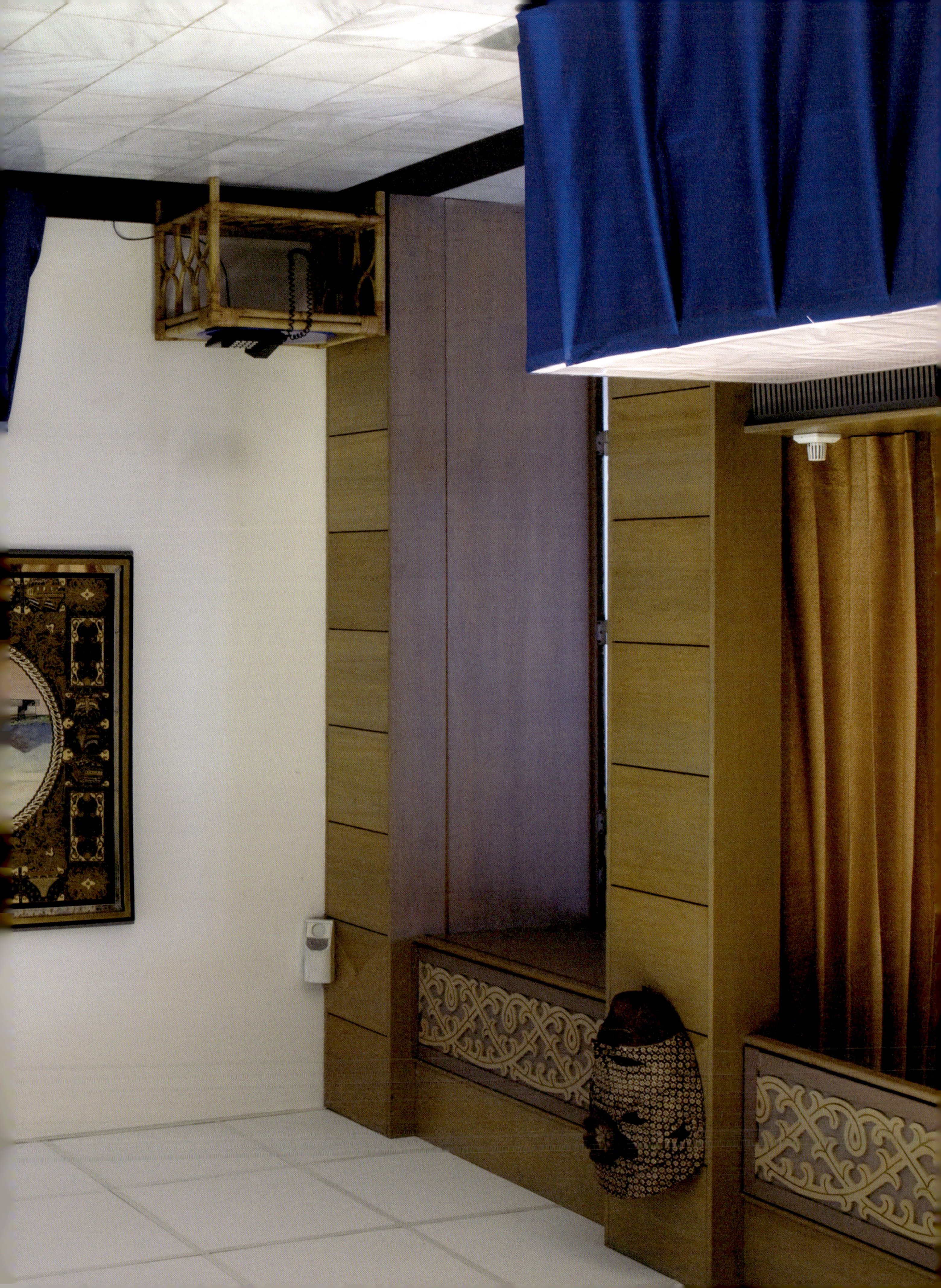

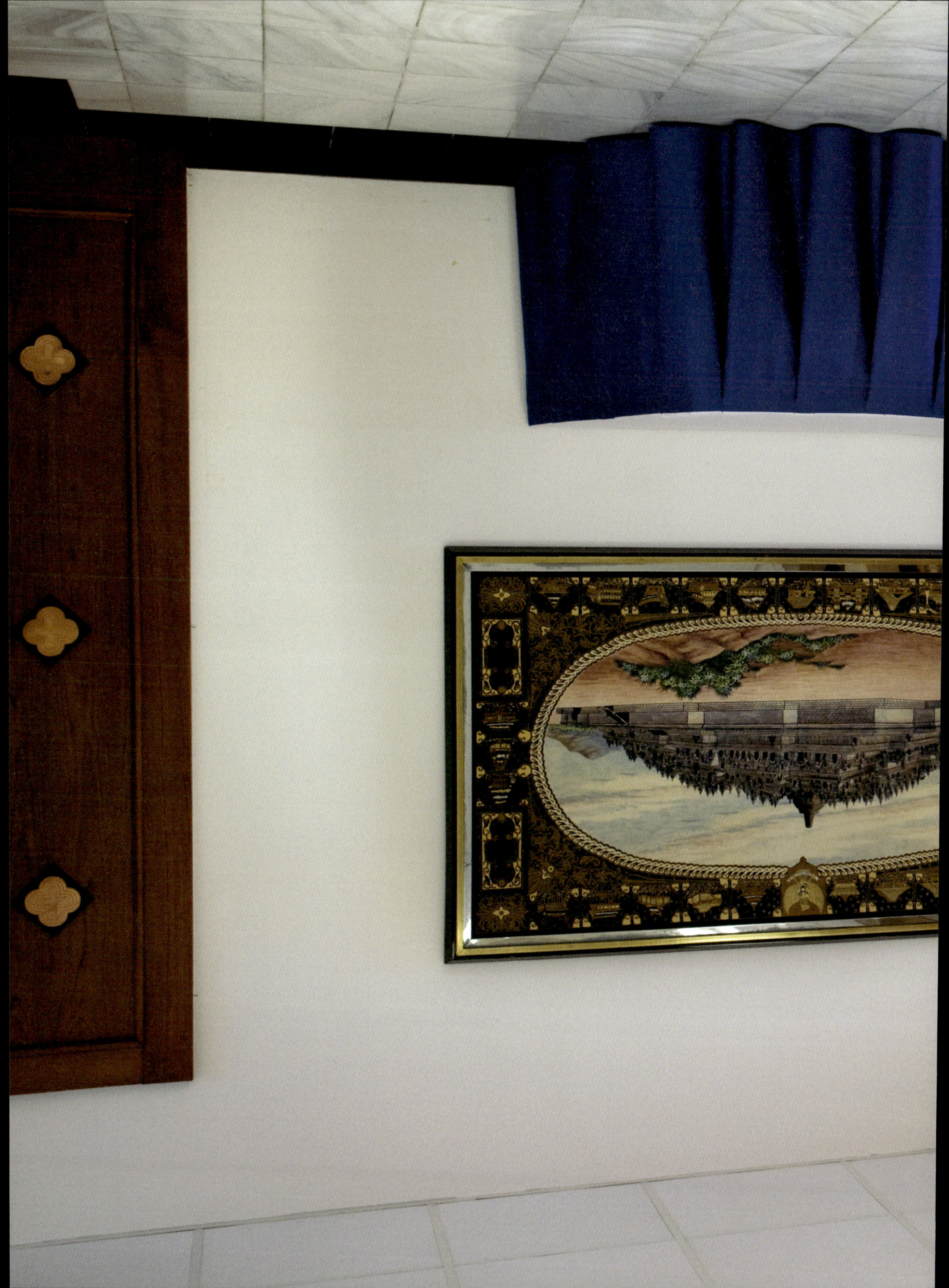

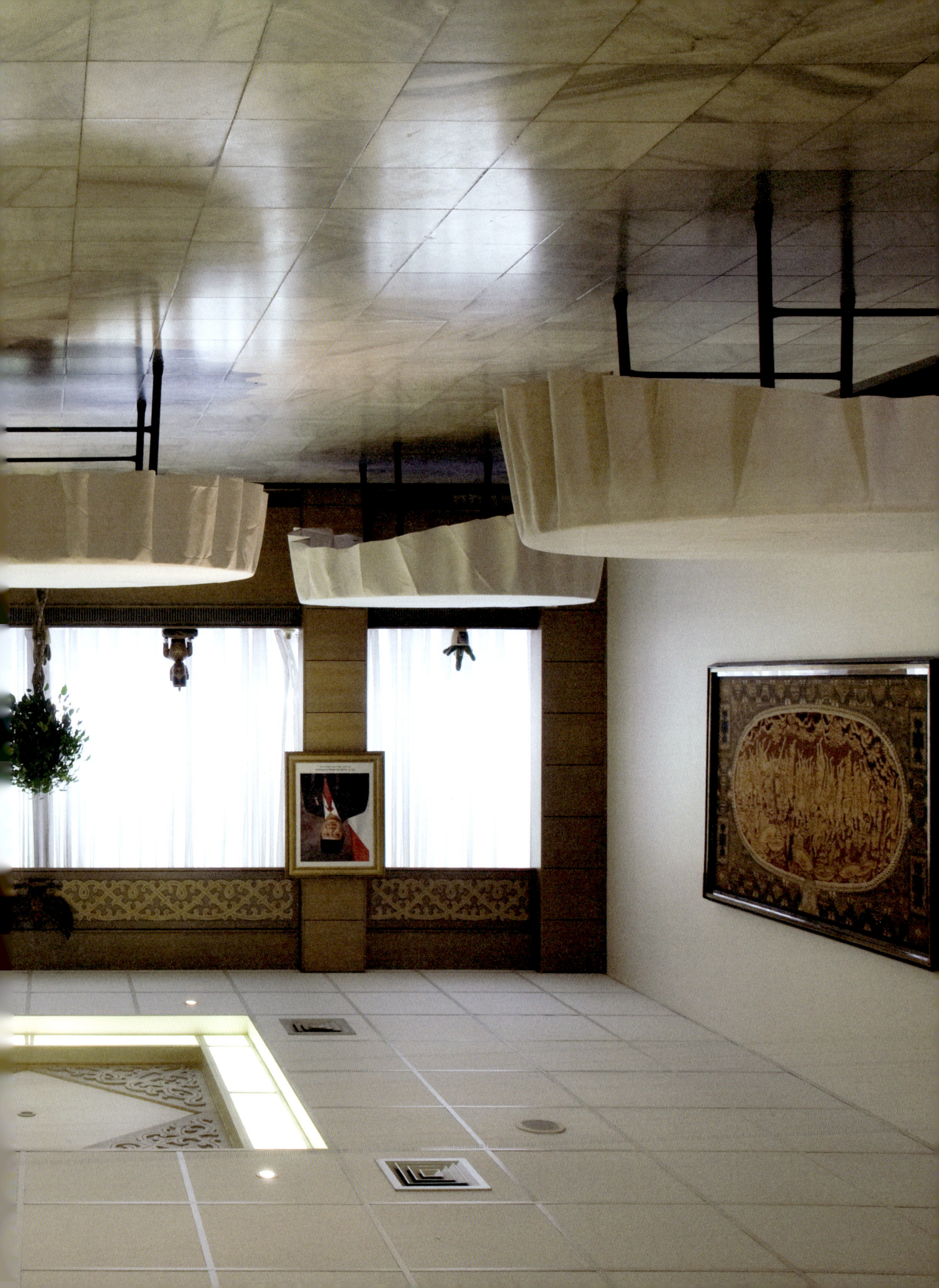

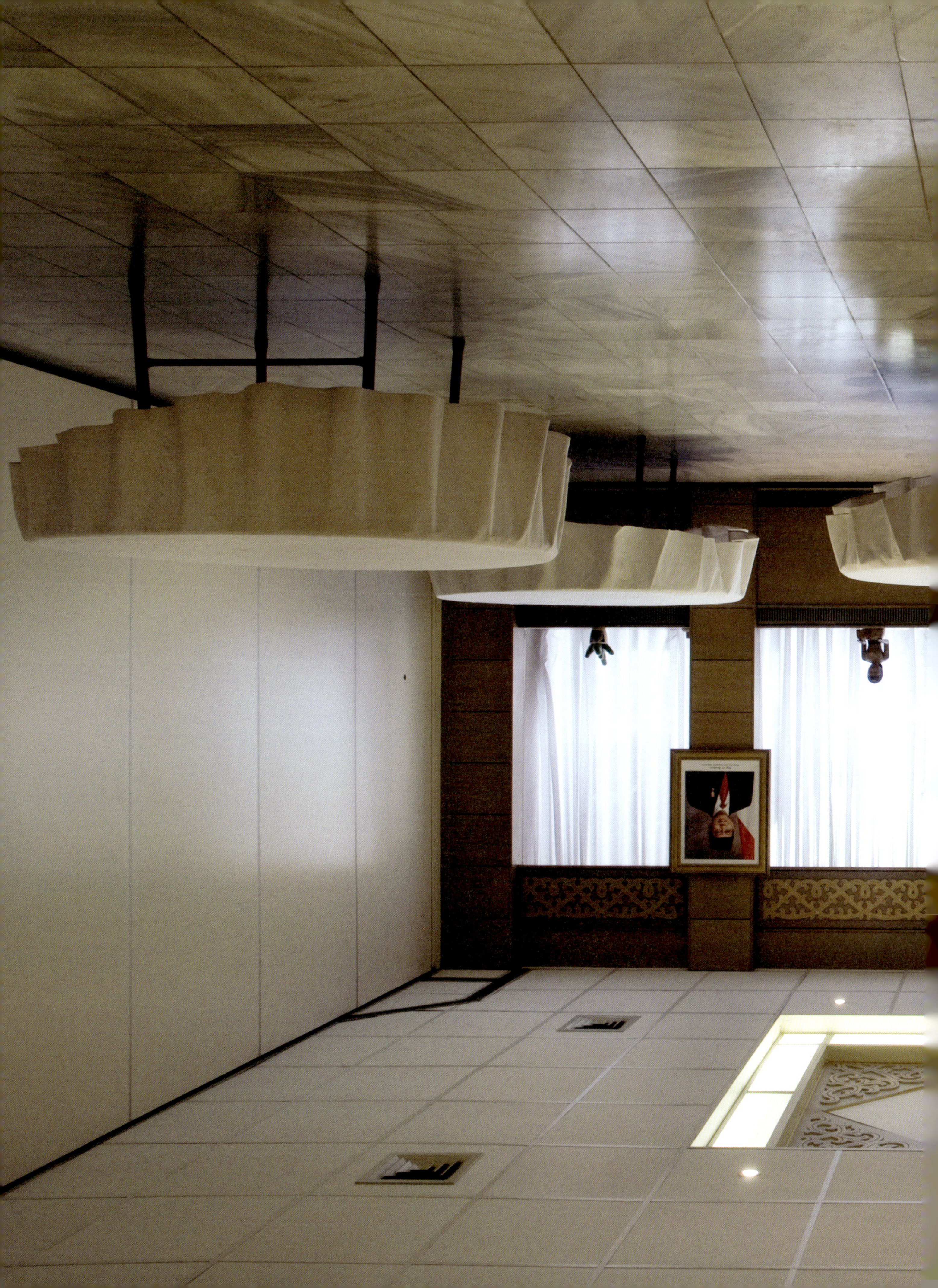

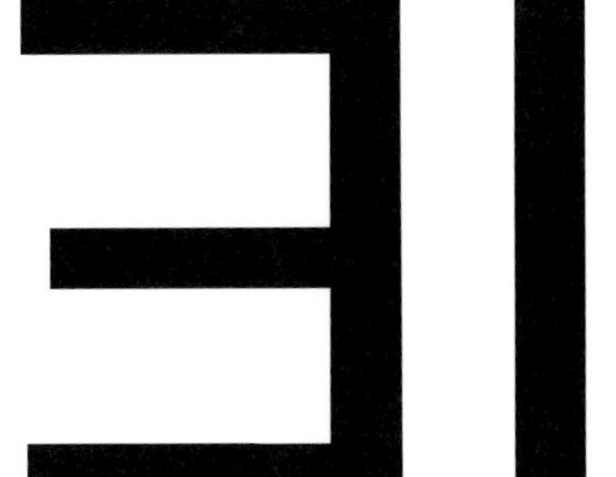

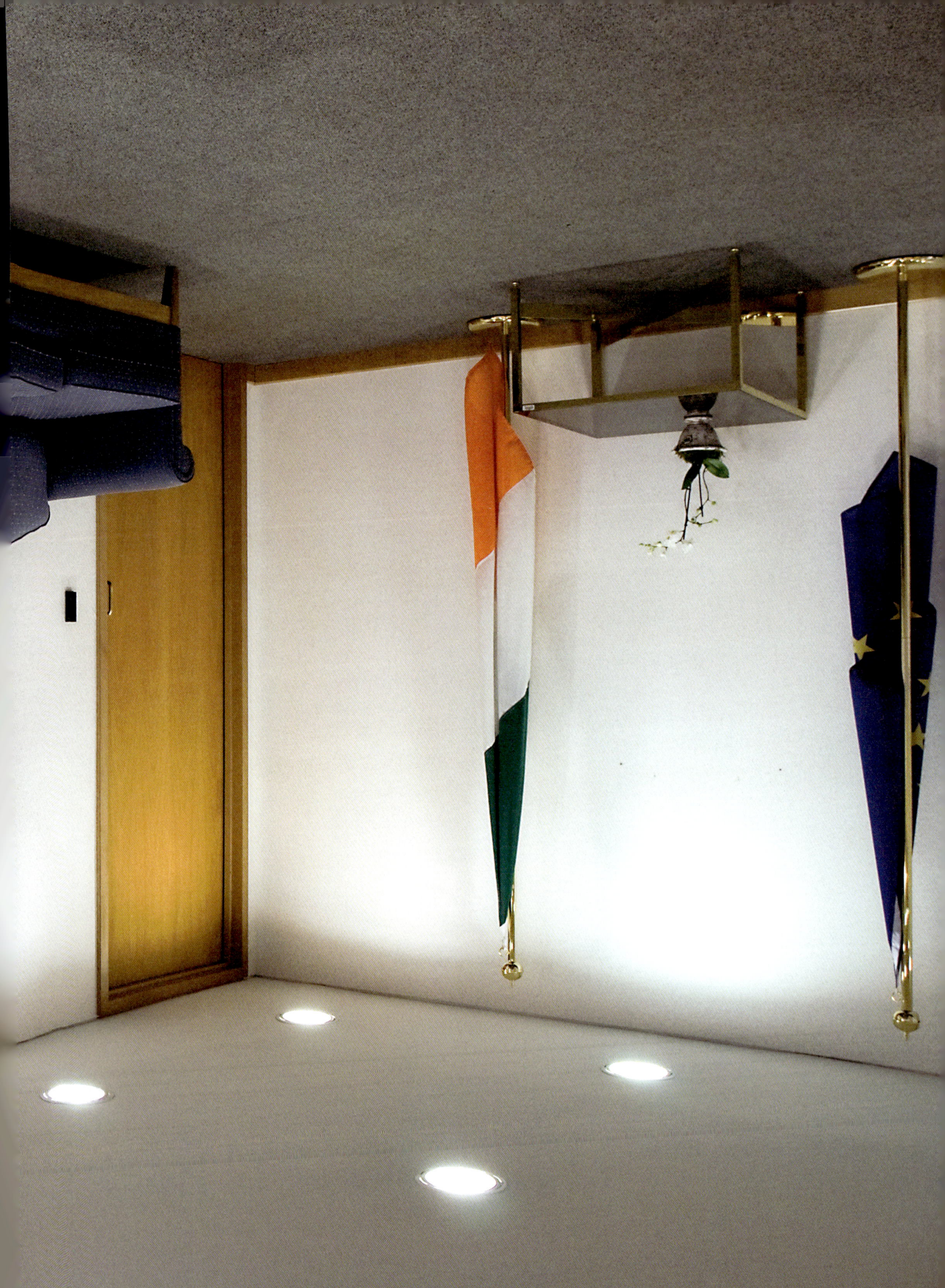

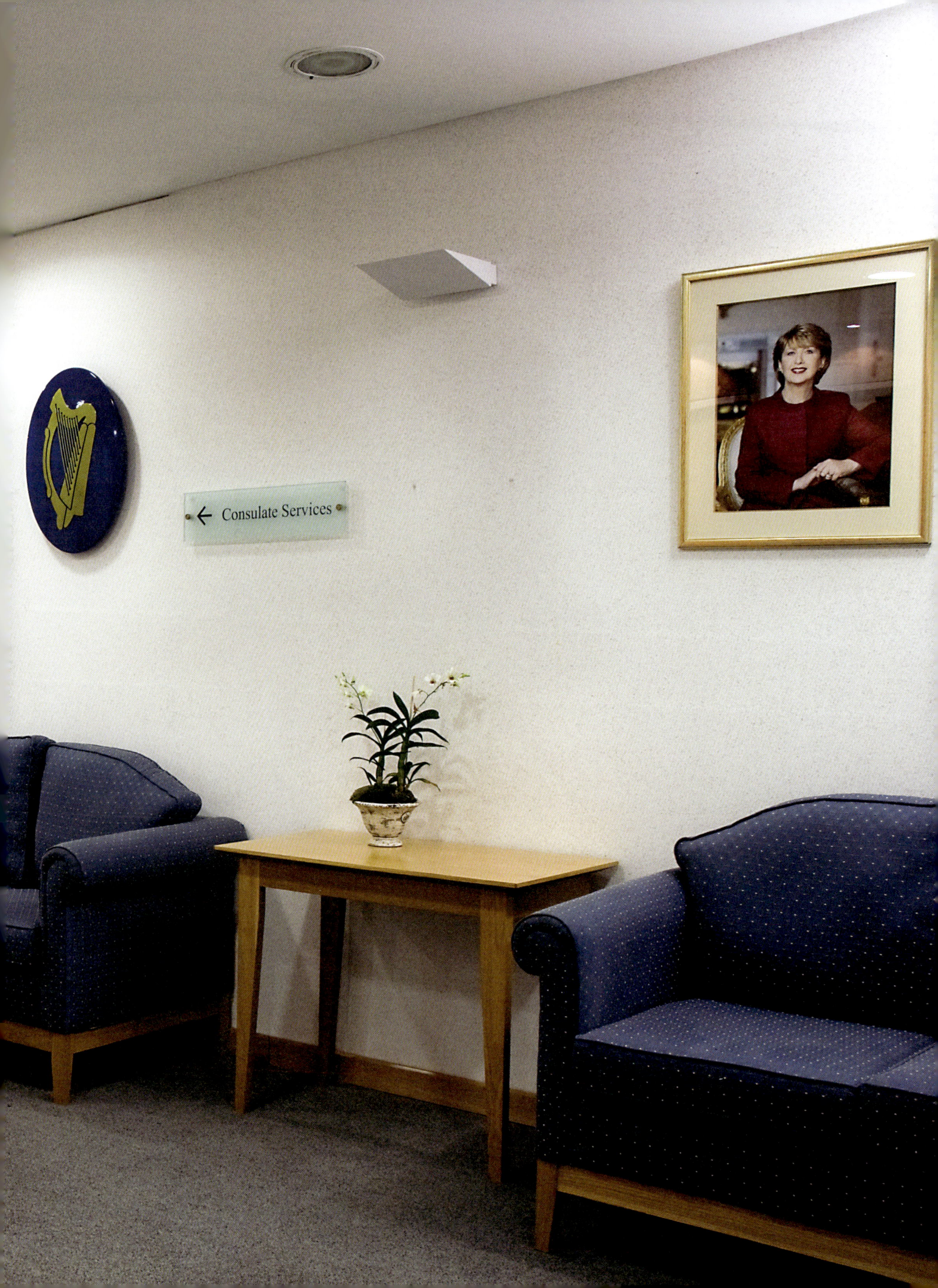
Consulate Services

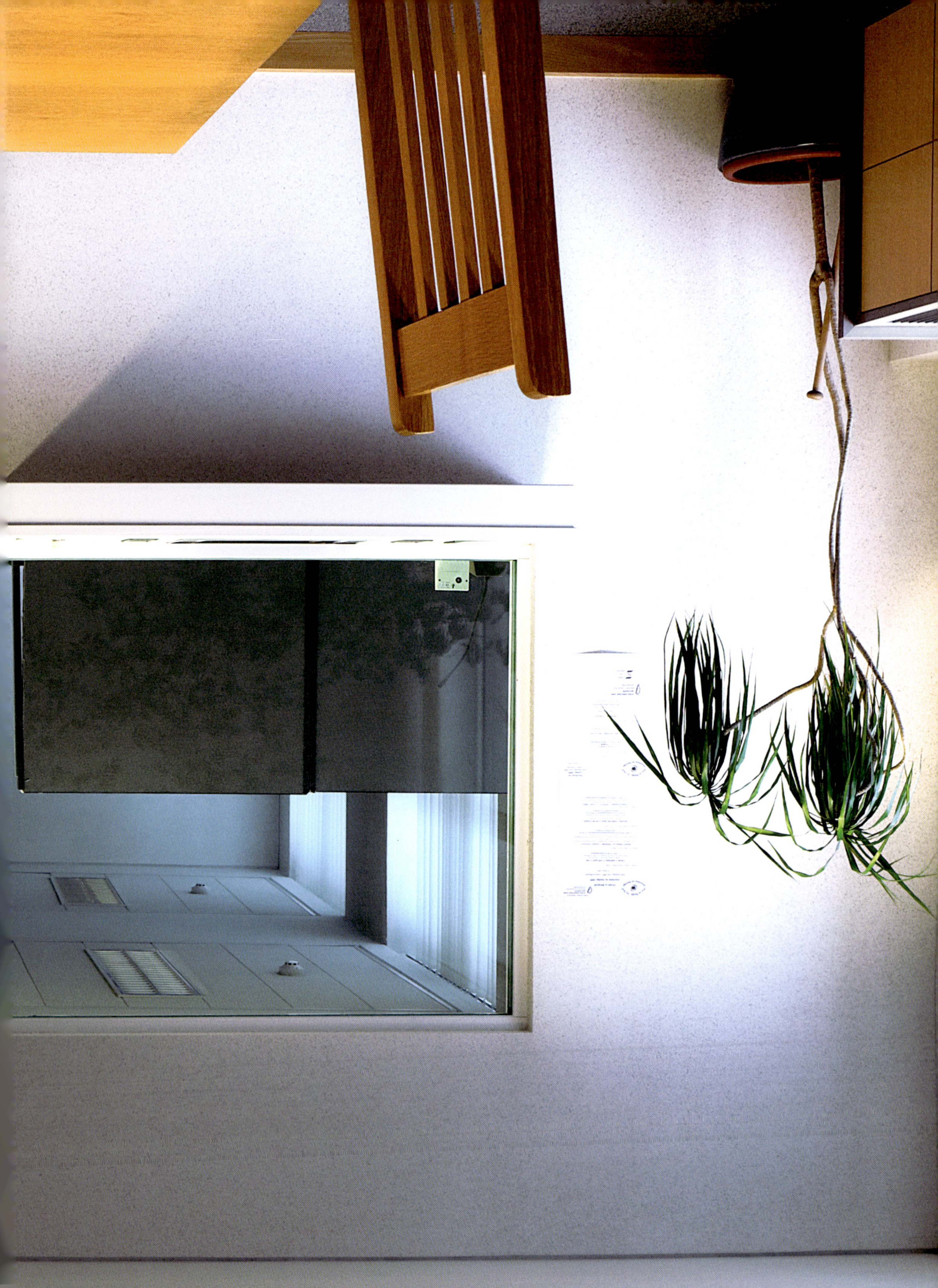

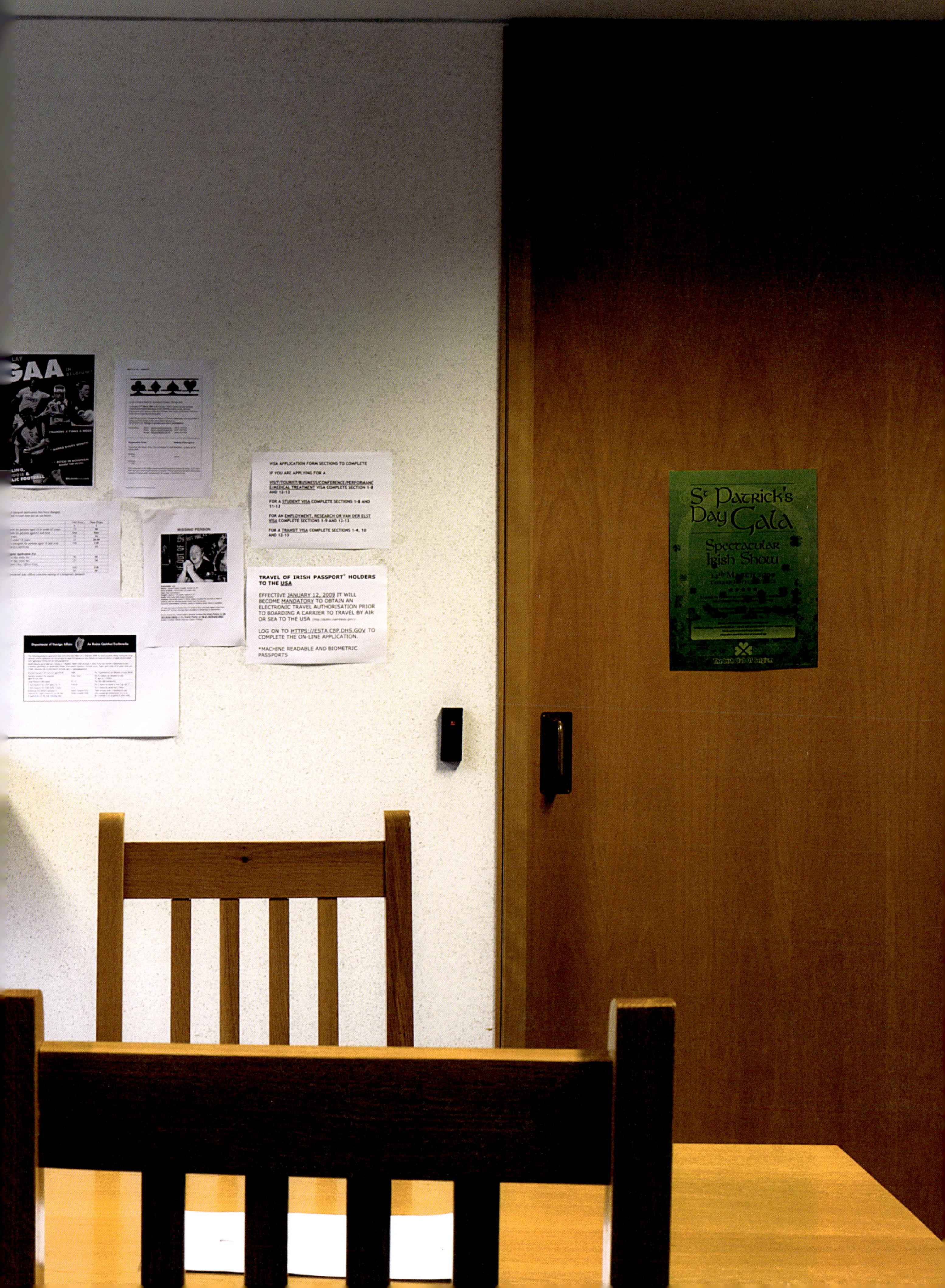
GAA
MISSING PERSON
VISA APPLICATION FORM SECTIONS TO COMPLETE
IF YOU ARE APPLYING FOR A
VISIT/TOURIST/BUSINESS/CONFERENCE/PERFORMANC E/MEDICAL TREATMENT VISA COMPLETE SECTION 1-8 AND 12-13
FOR A STUDENT VISA COMPLETE SECTIONS 1-8 AND 11-13
FOR AN EMPLOYMENT, RESEARCH OR VAN DER ELST VISA COMPLETE SECTIONS 1-9 AND 12-13
FOR A TRANSIT VISA COMPLETE SECTIONS 1-4, 10 AND 12-13
TRAVEL OF IRISH PASSPORT* HOLDERS TO THE USA
EFFECTIVE JANUARY 12, 2009 IT WILL BECOME MANDATORY TO OBTAIN AN ELECTRONIC TRAVEL AUTHORISATION PRIOR TO BOARDING A CARRIER TO TRAVEL BY AIR OR SEA TO THE USA
LOG ON TO HTTPS://ESTA.CBP.DHS.GOV TO COMPLETE THE ON-LINE APPLICATION.
*MACHINE READABLE AND BIOMETRIC PASSPORTS
Department of Foreign Affairs
St Patrick's Day Gala
Spectacular Irish Show

MT

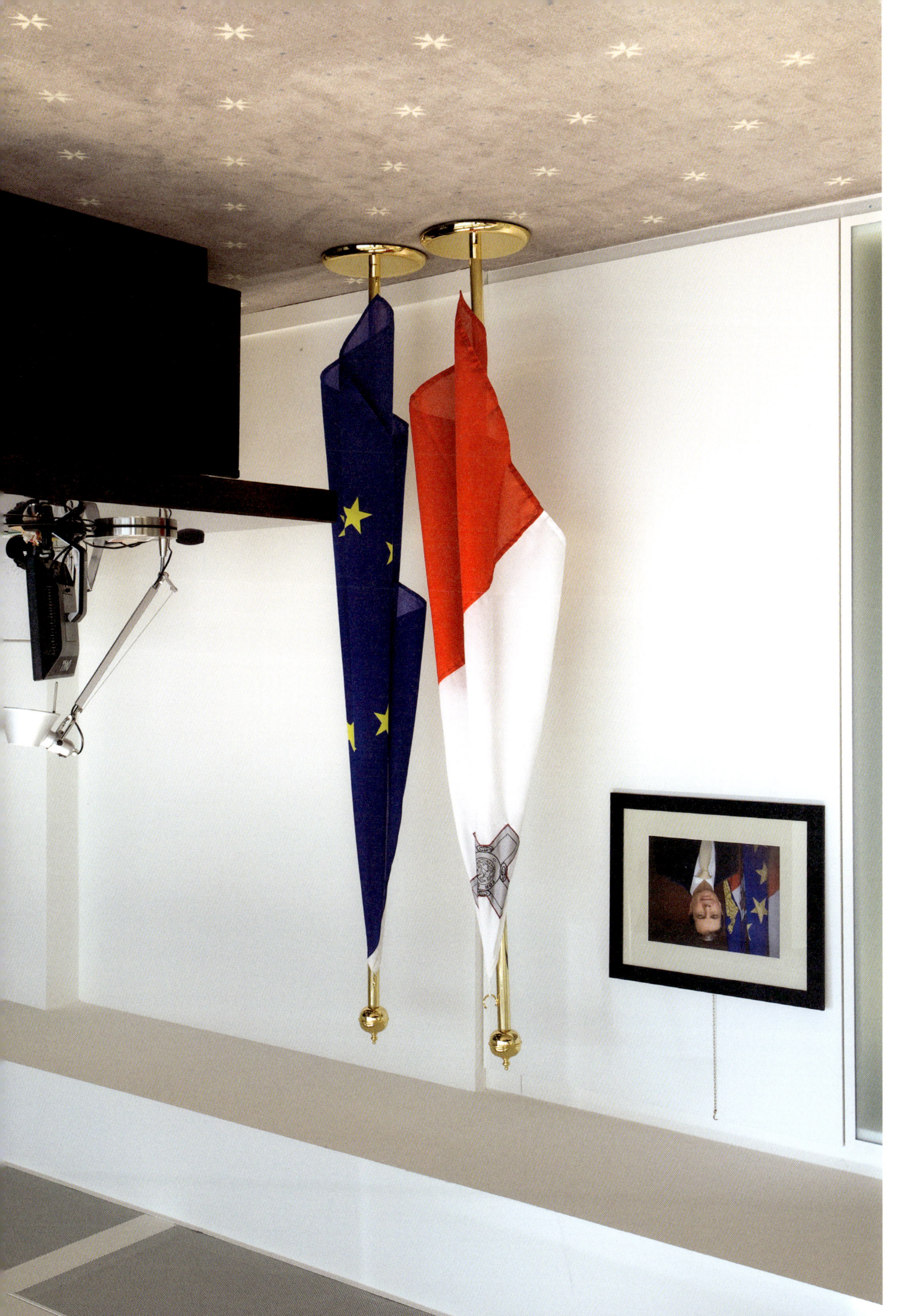

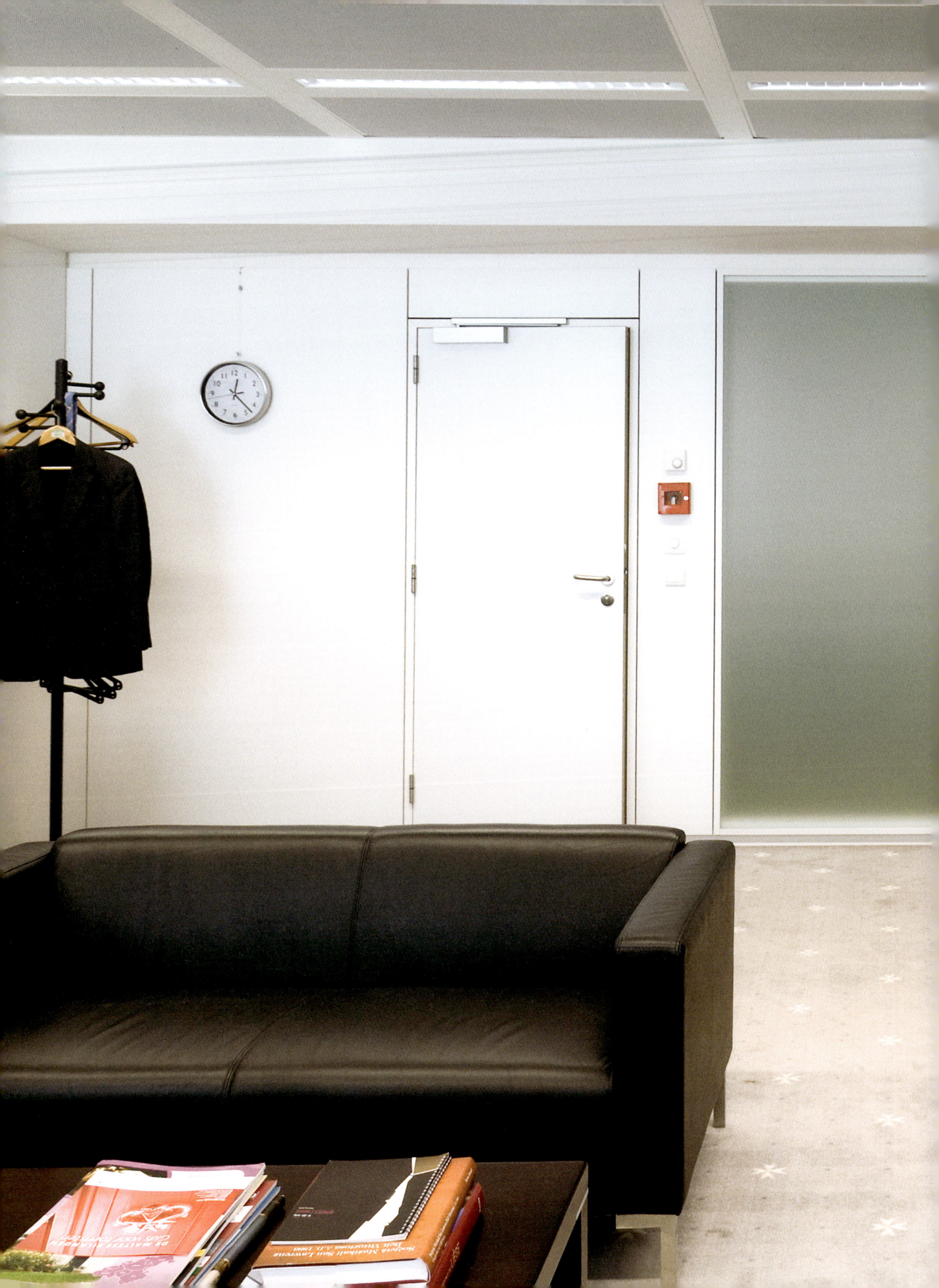
Soċjetà Mużikali San Lawrenz
Belt Vittoriosa

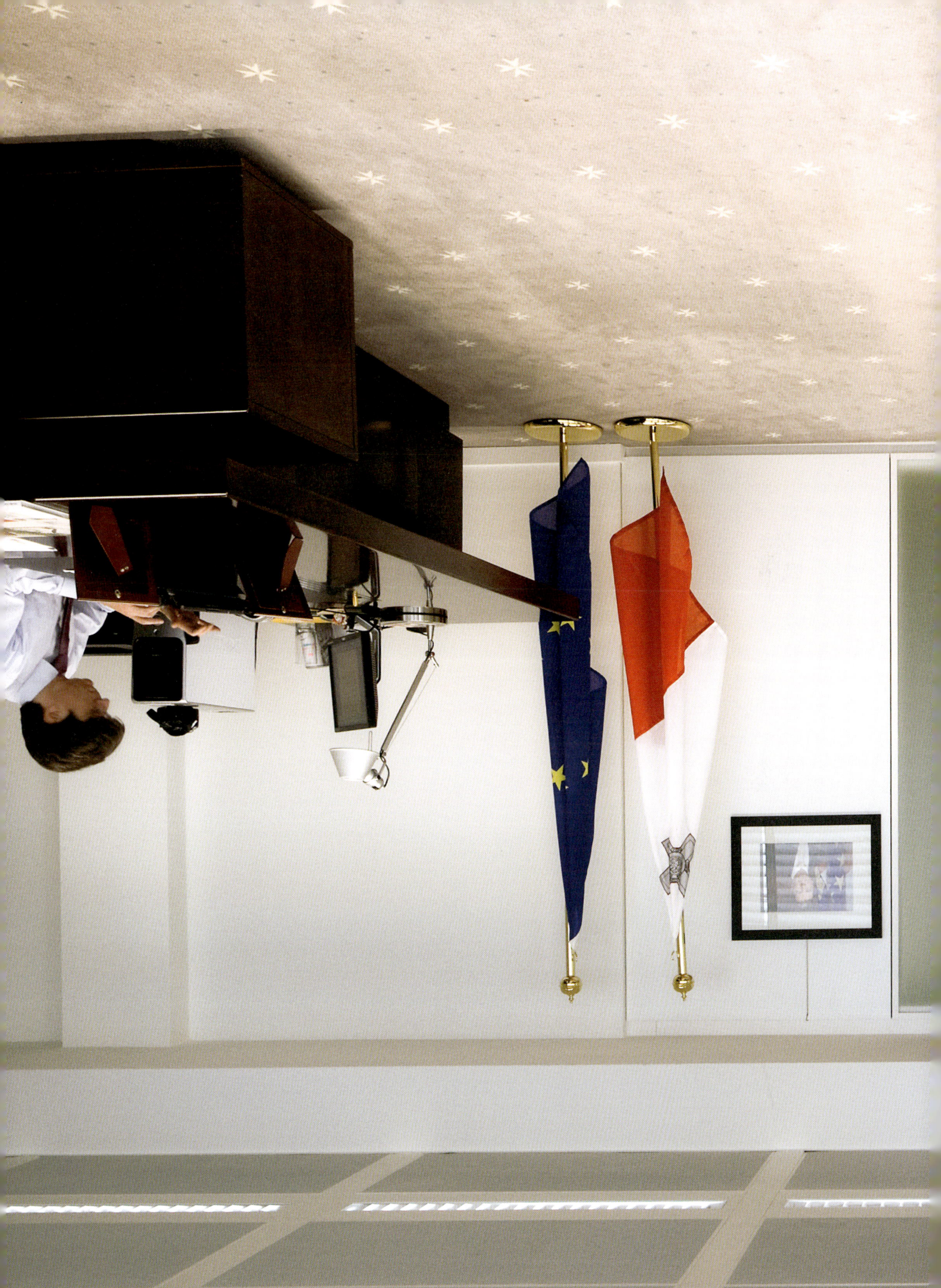

JM

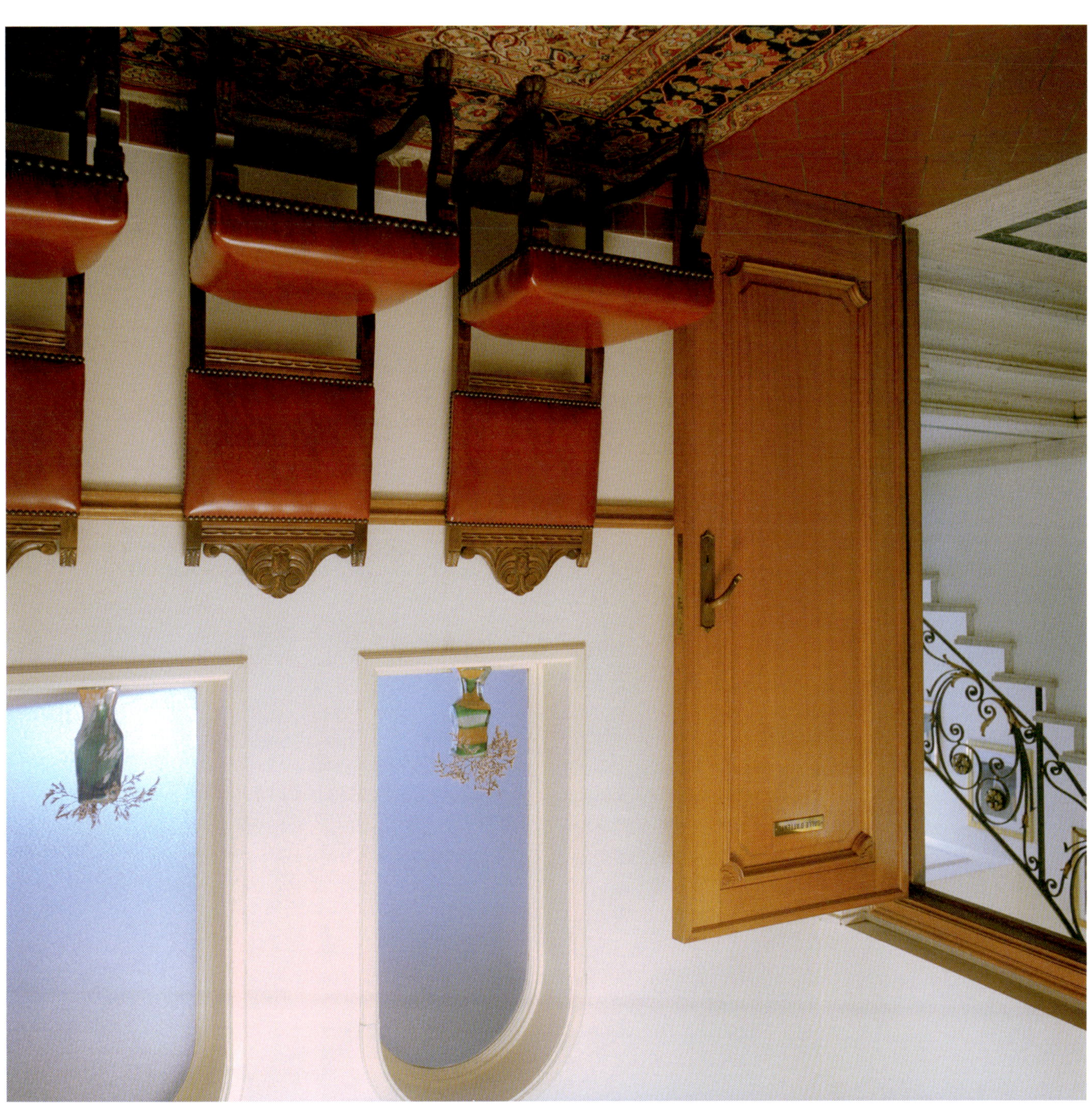

THE GAUCHE GATEWAY

An embassy is a gateway between two countries. But not one for which the key is readily handed out. Most bilateral ambassadors meet with only very select people in the country to which they are accredited. These can come from across a wide range of sectors (politics, business, the military, the arts, academia etc.) but for the most part they would be leaders in their fields, with sufficient influence to at the very least spread the positive image of the country to the public diplomacy of which they have just been subjected. Occasionally "young leaders" might be invited, reducing the average age of visitors to the embassy, but the public at large will rarely have that occasion.

Embassies therefore retain a certain mystique. As it is not very easy to visualise what diplomats really do all day, many still imagine a succession of lunches, dinners and receptions in gilded surroundings. An embassy, and diplomacy, do not so much stand for luxury as for elegance. Luxury can be found in any four star hotel, but not necessarily accompanied by the good taste that would make it worthwhile, especially not in those impersonal hotels that are branches of a major chain and where once inside the lobby one could be in any country in the world. Elegance on the contrary cannot be mass-produced. In that it is more of an art, which sees invitees moving about with savoir-faire in beautiful surroundings that express the identity of the country, engaging in discrete conversation, or exchanging indiscretions, while savouring the art works and design on display and the canapés on offer. These days the evening dress that comes with this Belle Epoque image of diplomacy rarely leaves the wardrobe however.

In reality, as Elisabeth Ida's photographs show, an embassy is first and foremost a place of work for the diplomats toiling there on what often are repetitive tasks, negotiating every word of a detailed technical agreement or drafting reports for the capital that might not be read but that are nonetheless expected. This side of diplomacy is associated more with dreary meeting rooms and drab offices than beautiful salons. Efforts made in waiting rooms, corridors and lobbies to convey something about the country while creating a certain homelike atmosphere come across as gauche rather than elegant. Sofas whose colour-scheme matches ill with the colours of the national flag give the impression of making do with what is available, under the watchful eye of the ubiquitous state picture of a president, king or queen, who are keen to ensure that the national budget is not wasted on undue comforts. The result appears strangely sterile and uninhabited, as if from a catalogue for budget-friendly diplomatic interior decoration.

Perhaps it can be somewhat of a consolation to know that behind the secured doors things are not always much better. For when the general public does enter an embassy, it usually is to spend many hours in the consular section, waiting for one's number to come up on the screen to present one's visa application or start some other administrative procedure. Elisabeth Ida thus shows us the normality of the embassy: daily life on both sides of the gateway goes on in pretty much the same way. The embassies who opened their doors for her certainly are to be commended for their transparency that allows us to glance at the less glamorous side of diplomacy.

Daily life can be enlivened however by beautiful occasions. What makes an occasion into an event that breaks the routine is that it does take place in beautiful surroundings, that one dresses up for it. Expecting something special, one will make a special effort. Ceremony and visual splendour serve a purpose. Thus the salon is as vital a part of embassy life as the office and the waiting room. But perhaps a few more people could be invited from time to time and take part in what remains a fascinating and, for those engaged in it, passionate profession: diplomacy.

Prof. Dr. Sven Biscop
Ghent University & Egmont – Royal Institute for International Relations (Brussels)

MX

ELISABETH IDA MULYANI
INSIDE EMBASSIES